WONDERFUL WORLD OF KNOWLEDGE

YEAR BOOK 1991

Disney's

Wonderful World of Knowledge

YEAR BOOK 1991

GROLIER ENTERPRISES, INC.
Danbury, Connecticut

FERN L. MAMBERG   *Executive Editor*

MICHÈLE A. MCLEAN   *Art Director*

MARILYN SMITH   *Production Manager*

ISBN 0-7172-8255-4
The Library of Congress Catalog Card Number: 78-66149

CONTENTS

1990 AT A GLANCE

JANUARY 7. It was reported that recently discovered dinosaur fossils may disprove the long-held theory that *Tyrannosaurus rex* was the largest meat-eating dinosaur. The fossils, found in Colorado, were of a dinosaur named *Epanterias amplexus*. They indicated that this dinosaur was as big as the biggest *tyrannosaur*. *Epanterias* lived 30 million years before the *tyrannosaur*. It weighed about four tons and was nearly twice as long as a school bus. Its jaws were expandable, like those of a snake, allowing it to eat an animal as big as a cow in a single gulp.

JANUARY 20. The space shuttle *Columbia* completed the longest mission in the history of the shuttle program, returning to Earth after almost eleven days in space. One of the mission's highlights was the retrieval of a failing scientific satellite, which was brought back to Earth in *Columbia*'s cargo bay.

JANUARY 24. Japan launched a rocket with two satellites to the moon. Previously, only the United States and the Soviet Union had sent spacecraft to the moon. The satellites were released into lunar orbit for scientific observations.

FEBRUARY 9. It was reported that scientists had identified the world's oldest known flowering plant. Called the Koonwarra plant, it was an herb about an inch (2.5 centimeters) tall. Its tiny flower was probably greenish or beige. The plant lived 120 million years ago and is known only through fossils found in the Koonwarra area of southeastern Australia. It is believed that almost all of today's flowering plants are descendants of the Koonwarra plant.

FEBRUARY 11. Nelson Mandela, the South African black nationalist leader who spent 27 years in jail for his efforts to end white minority rule in his country, was freed. During his years in prison, Mandela had helped focus worldwide attention on the struggle for racial equality in South Africa. Free at last, the 71-year-old Mandela faced a difficult task: to work with both black and white leaders to find a solution to the racial strife that has long divided South Africa.

MARCH 21. Namibia, Africa's last territory, became an independent nation, ending 75 years of South African rule.

APRIL 22. Millions of people throughout the world participated in Earth Day festivities. The event, which marked the 20th anniversary of the first Earth Day, was celebrated by parades, concerts, marches, clean-up campaigns, workshops, and other activities designed to increase people's awareness of environmental issues.

APRIL 29. The space shuttle *Discovery* completed a five-day mission. The mission's highlight was the launch of the Hubble Space Telescope, a $1.5 billion instrument designed to give people the clearest view yet of the far reaches of the universe. (On June 27, scientists reported that the telescope's main mirror was flawed. As a result, the telescope wasn't sharply focusing incoming light, and its images weren't as clear as expected. This limited the ability of the telescope to study distant objects. But in spite of its fuzzy focus, the Hubble was able to produce spectacular views of the heavens, sending back pictures that were better than those produced by ground-based telescopes.)

JUNE 3. U.S. President George Bush and Soviet President Mikhail Gorbachev ended a four-day summit meeting in Washington, D.C. It was their second summit meeting. The two leaders signed an agreement to end production of chemical weapons and eliminate most of their existing stockpiles. They also approved the framework of a new treaty to reduce strategic (long-range) nuclear weapons.

JUNE 11. The U.S. Supreme Court ruled that a recently passed Federal law making it a crime to burn or deface the American flag was unconstitutional. The justices said that the law suppressed freedom of speech, which is protected under the First Amendment. The Federal law had been passed following a public outcry over a 1989 Supreme Court ruling that struck down a Texas law against flag burning, also because it violated First Amendment guarantees.

JULY 20. U.S. Supreme Court Justice William J. Brennan, Jr., resigned. He had served on the Court for nearly 34 years and was considered the leader of the liberal members. (On July 23, President George Bush nominated David H. Souter, a judge on the Federal Court of Appeals in Boston, to succeed Brennan.

JULY 26. It was reported that a team of U.S. archeologists had discovered a tiny statue that was once an ancient figure of worship. Said to be an example of the biblical "golden calf," it is believed to be about 3,500 years old and the only one of its kind ever found. Such idols were worshipped in Canaan, an ancient land between the Mediterranean Sea and the Jordan River. The calf figurine was discovered during excavations of Canaanite ruins near Ashkelon, Israel. The calf is about the size of a human hand. And it is made primarily of bronze, rather than gold—it was probably kept polished to a high sheen so that it looked like gold.

AUGUST 2. Iraqi troops invaded the neighboring nation of Kuwait and seized control of the country and its rich oilfields. The Kuwaiti government headed by Sheik Jabir al-Ahmad al-Sabah fled to Saudi Arabia. The following day, Iraqi troops moved into position for a possible attack on Saudi Arabia. On August 6, the United Nations Security Council voted to impose a trade embargo on Iraq and occupied Kuwait. On August 7, President George Bush ordered American troops to Saudi Arabia to defend its oilfields from Iraqi attack. On August 8, Iraq declared that it had annexed Kuwait, a move declared "null and void" by the U.N. Security Council the next day. During the following weeks, other nations—including Britain, France, Syria, and Egypt—sent troops to Saudi Arabia. On August 25, the U.N. Security Council voted to allow the use of force to halt shipping to and from Iraq, in order to prevent violations of the trade embargo. By the end of the month, most of the nations of the world were united in condemning the Iraqi invasion.

SEPTEMBER 9. U.S. President George Bush and Soviet leader Mikhail Gorbachev met in Helsinki, Finland, to discuss Iraq's invasion of Kuwait. The two leaders agreed "that Iraq's aggression must not be tolerated" but that they hoped to resolve the crisis peacefully.

SEPTEMBER 30. More than 70 presidents, prime ministers, and other world leaders gathered at the United Nations in New York City for the World Summit for Children. It was the largest gathering of government leaders in modern times. The purpose of the meeting was to focus world attention on the plight of young people, especially children in the poorer countries and in the inner cities of industrialized nations. The leaders agreed to work together to fight disease, malnutrition, and illiteracy among children.

OCTOBER 3. After 45 years of separation, West Germany and East Germany were reunited into a single nation. In effect, East Germany was absorbed into West Germany, and the East German government went out of existence. Berlin became the capital of the new Federal Republic of Germany. West German leaders kept their posts in the new government.

OCTOBER 24. Elizabeth H. Dole resigned as U.S. Secretary of Labor. (On December 14, Lynn Martin was named to succeed Dole.)

NOVEMBER 22. President George Bush spent Thanksgiving visiting some of the 230,000 American troops in Saudi Arabia. In his speeches, Bush stressed that the United States was prepared to use force to oust Iraqi troops that had invaded neighboring Kuwait in August.

NOVEMBER 27. In Britain, the ruling Conservative Party chose John Major to be its new leader and the nation's prime minister. Major succeeded Margaret Thatcher, who resigned after having been prime minister since 1979.

NOVEMBER 29. The United Nations Security Council voted to allow the United States and its allies to oust Iraq from Kuwait by force if Iraqi troops weren't withdrawn by January 15, 1991.

DECEMBER 1. Deep below the English Channel, French and British construction workers shook hands, to celebrate the breakthrough of the Channel Tunnel. Popularly known as the "Chunnel," the 30-mile (48-kilometer) tunnel will connect Folkestone, England, and Coquelles, France, when it is completed in 1993. It will cut travel time between London and Paris from 12 hours to only 3 hours. The Chunnel will actually contain three tunnels. The tunnel where the breakthrough occurred will be used for maintenance. Two other tunnels will carry trains—one for traffic toward England, the other for traffic toward France.

DECEMBER 12. Lauro F. Cavazos resigned as Secretary of Education. (On December 17, Lamar Alexander was named to succeed Cavazos.)

Clownfish and sea anemones are partners in a special relationship that benefits both animals. These partnerships are common in nature, and they help animals to survive.

ANIMAL PARTNERS

Sea anemones are animals that look like flowers, with dozens of brightly colored tentacles that wave about in the water. The tentacles deliver a deadly poisonous sting—and when an unfortunate fish blunders into them, it's usually killed and eaten by the anemone. But one fish is an exception to this rule: clownfish live right among the tentacles without being harmed.

Sea anemones and clownfish are partners in a relationship that benefits both animals. The clownfish cleans away debris from among the anemone's tentacles. And this debris is often food for the clownfish. In addition, the relationship gives the fish protection: Few predators will risk the anemone's sting to pursue them.

How does the clownfish avoid being

stung? Before it tries to swim among an anemone's tentacles, the clownfish will brush lightly against the anemone. It does this repeatedly, quickly swimming away each time. Scientists think that by doing this, the fish builds up an immunity to the anemone's poison. But the fish must remember which anemone to go back to—if it swims into the wrong one, it won't be immune.

The sea anemone and the clownfish are far from unique in their teamwork. Partnerships between two different kinds of animals are common in nature. They are called *symbiotic relationships*. And these partnerships help both animals to survive.

CLEANERS

Many animal partnerships, like that of the anemone and the clownfish, are based on the exchange of cleaning services for food and other benefits. And a great many of these relationships involve fish and other water

The little cleaner wrasse at right and the cleaner shrimp below aren't afraid of their big partners. They specialize in clearing away parasites and other debris from the larger fish—and they get a free meal in the process.

creatures. Most of these animals can't groom themselves the way cats, monkeys, and many other land animals do. They depend on other creatures to do it for them.

The cleaner wrasse is a specialist in this job. These small fish are brightly colored, which makes them easy to spot. They set up cleaning stations in the ocean and attract clients with a sort of dance, swimming head down and waving their bodies from side to side.

Larger fish line up at the cleaner wrasse station, each waiting for its turn to be cleaned. The cleaners' clients include many fish that are predators—but the cleaners themselves are rarely eaten. As the larger fish wait calmly, the little cleaners swim right into their mouths and gill cavities to clear away parasites, fungi, and debris, getting a free meal in the process.

Many other ocean creatures perform cleaning services. One of them is the remora, or suckerfish. This bold fish travels with the shark, one of the most feared ocean preda-

tors. The remora has a large sucker on top of its head with which it attaches itself firmly to the shark. (Some remoras attach themselves to other large ocean creatures, even whales.) As the shark swims along, the remora travels all over its body removing debris. It gets food and protection—and an occasional feast. Sharks are messy eaters, and when the shark feeds, the remora detaches itself and gobbles up the leftover bits.

An unusual animal partnership is that of the huge sperm whale and a small shore bird, the gray phalarope. The sperm whale is a mammal and must come to the surface to breathe. When it does, part of its huge body breaks the surface of the water for a few seconds. The little phalarope swoops down, lands on the whale's back, and quickly pecks up parasites before the whale dives again. Phalaropes normally live near the shores of Africa and Latin America. But they have been known to follow whales far out to sea.

One of the strangest partnerships involves the Nile crocodile and a bird called the

The cattle egret is often seen hopping around the feet of large animals such as rhinos. The grazing animal helps the egret catch its food, and the egret warns the large animal of danger.

Egyptian plover. The crocodile cruises the muddy waters of African rivers and lakes. As it does so, leeches and other pests fasten onto the soft tissues of its mouth. Bits of food become trapped between its teeth.

This reptile is also a fearsome predator, up to 12 feet (3.6 meters) long, with sharp teeth and huge, powerful jaws. Most animals keep a sharp lookout for the crocodile and avoid it. But when the Egyptian plover spots a crocodile sunning itself on a riverbank, with its jaws gaping wide open, the bird hops right into the croc's open mouth! Does the crocodile eat the bird? No. Instead of snapping up what would seem at first glance to be a free snack, the crocodile just lies there as the bird hops in its mouth and removes the leeches and debris, giving the croc a free tooth-cleaning. In return, the bird gets a meal. The bird also acts as a lookout for the crocodile as it naps on the riverbank. And for as long as the cleaning goes on, the bird has the protection of this powerful predator.

FEATHERED FRIENDS

Birds like the Egyptian plover are involved in partnerships with animals of many kinds. In the Mediterranean Sea, for example, several kinds of gulls get help with housecleaning chores from the common wall lizard.

The birds build their nests in crevices along the rocky shores of islands. Insect pests soon move in, troubling parent and young birds alike. But wall lizards clamber among the nests, eating the insects. The lizards are just the right size to make a meal for the gulls—but the birds ignore them as they go about their job.

Other birds work in partnership with grazing animals. One of the most familiar of these is the cattle egret. In Africa, this elegant white bird can be seen hopping around the feet of antelope, zebras, elephants, and other large animals. But it has expanded its range to the Americas, where it is often seen among herds of cattle.

The grazing animals help the egret catch its food—insects, especially grasshoppers. As the animals move through the grass, insects hiding there are disturbed and pop up into the air. The egret spots them and gobbles them up. In exchange, the egret warns the grazing herd of approaching dan-

17

Cleaning services, in return for food, are also provided by the oxpecker. This little bird spends almost its entire life riding around on the back of a large animal, feeding on the ticks that it finds there.

ger—by hopping up on an animal's back, calling, and flapping its wings. If the animal is slow to respond, the egret will even peck on its head to get its attention.

Egrets also perform some cleaning services for grazing animals, removing insect pests from their coats. But another bird—the oxpecker—is a specialist in this job. Oxpeckers live in Africa, where they spend almost their entire lives riding around on the backs of large animals, such as warthogs and buffalo. The birds sleep, sunbathe, and even mate on the animals' backs. Their main food consists of the ticks that they find there and remove. The birds leave their hosts only to nest or, briefly, if they are disturbed. Like cattle egrets, oxpeckers will warn their host animal of danger, drumming on its head to make it hurry away.

Cowbirds are native to North America, where they live with herds of cattle. Like cattle egrets, they keep the animals free of insect pests and feed on insects kicked up by the animals. Cowbirds once followed the great herds of bison that roamed across the North American plains. Because the herds were constantly on the move, the birds developed an unusual way of raising their young: Cowbirds lay their eggs in other birds' nests, leaving the job of hatching and raising the young to an unsuspecting stranger.

ALLIES IN DEFENSE

If you've seen films of animals grazing on the plains of Africa, you may have noticed that some kinds of animals seem to hang around together. Ostriches can often be spotted near herds of zebras. Around waterholes, impala often can be found with baboons. The animals may seem to be ignoring each other, but they are actually working together for mutual protection.

Zebras and ostriches, for example, help alert each other to the approach of predators. The ostrich has excellent eyesight, and its long neck helps it see far away. It may spot enemies before the zebra can. But the zebra has an excellent sense of smell. It may scent enemies before the ostrich can see them. By working together, the animals increase their chances of escaping.

The graceful impala is the favorite prey of

lions and many other fierce predators. Luckily, it's also one of the most alert of the African creatures, with sharp senses of sight, hearing, and smell. And its association with baboons helps both animals. When a lion begins to creep up on the animals at a waterhole, the impala alert the baboons. And the baboons are large and fierce enough to drive off most predators—including lions.

Many ocean animals also team up for defense. One of these partnerships involves certain crabs and sponges. The crab—called, appropriately, the sponge crab—looks around until it finds the right kind of sponge. Then the crab uses its claws to snip off a piece of the sponge. It puts the sponge on top of its shell, holding it there with its hind legs. The sponge grows along with the crab, until it covers the crab's shell completely. This hides the crab from predators.

The sponge isn't just along for the ride. Sponges are filter feeders—that is, they filter tiny particles of food from the water. As the crab moves along the ocean floor, water currents pass through the sponge and provide a constant supply of food.

Other crabs team up with anemones. The pom-pom crab, for example, carries anemones in its claws. If an enemy approaches, the crab stretches out its claws and threatens the attacker with an anemone sting. The anemones benefit because the crab carries them to new, richer feeding grounds—on their own, anemones can move only very slowly. The anemones also may be able to pick up some scraps from the crab's meals—crabs are messy eaters.

Hermit crabs also make use of the poisonous sting of anemones. These crabs adopt the abandoned shells of other sea creatures as their homes, and it's not uncommon to see a hermit crab scuttling around in a shell that's coverered with anemones. There may be as many as eight anemones traveling with a single crab! With friends like these, the hermit crab is safe from most predators, and the anemones get a free ride to fresh feeding grounds.

Many ocean animals team up for defense. The sponge crab carries a sponge on top of its shell. The sponge hides the crab from predators, and it gets a constant supply of food in return.

Some crabs have partnerships with anemones for defense. The pom-pom crab above carries anemones in its claws. The hermit crab at right blankets itself with an abandoned shell covered with anemones. In both cases, the slow-moving anemones catch free rides to new feeding grounds.

SWEET TEAMWORK

Some animal partnerships are formed to satisfy a craving for something sweet to eat. The best known of these is probably the relationship between ants and aphids.

Aphids are tiny insects that excrete a sweet, sticky substance called honeydew. You can sometimes see dried honeydew on plant leaves, glistening in the sun. Aphids suck the juices from the plants that they live on, so gardeners consider them to be pests. But ants love aphids—because ants love honeydew.

Several kinds of ants have developed ways of keeping herds of aphids, much as people keep herds of cows. They collect aphids and bring them to a plant near their nest, so that honeydew will always be handy. Whenever an ant wants honeydew, it "milks" an aphid by tapping or stroking it. This prompts the aphid to release the sweet substance. In exchange, the ants protect the aphids.

Some ants go even further. The ants of one species build small mud shelters for their aphids and herd them inside at night, protecting them from predators and harsh weather. Those of other species take their aphids into their own nests for the night. In the morning, the aphids are taken outside to feed on plant juices.

Some kinds of ants have also developed

partnerships with other insects. In Australia, ants called meat ants wait for the eggs of the imperial blue butterfly to hatch. When the butterfly larvae crawl out, the ants follow them around and protect them, using vicious bites to fight off predators. At first the ants receive nothing in return. But as the larvae grow into larger caterpillars, they begin to produce honeydew. Then the ants can milk them just as they milk aphids.

When the time comes for a caterpillar to change into a butterfly, it pupates and forms a chrysalis. During this dormant time, the ants guard it once again. But when it emerges as a full-grown butterfly, it must fly away quickly. At this stage the ants forget their partnership and will attack it.

The large blue butterfly of Europe and Asia has a similar partnership with ants. But the relationship is even closer. Red ants will take a blue butterfly caterpillar right into their nest. There they keep it supplied with food in exchange for honeydew. The ants will even feed their own newly hatched larvae to the hungry caterpillar.

The caterpillar pupates right in the nest, where it is safe. Scientists who have studied this partnership have discovered that large blue butterflies can't reproduce without the help of the red ants—the caterpillars don't seem to be able to pupate outside the ants' nest.

A fondness for sweet things is also the basis of a very different kind of animal partnership—the partnership between a bird called the black-throated honey guide and the honey badger, or ratel. Both these creatures live in Africa and parts of Asia.

The honey guide likes to eat the beeswax and larvae that are inside bees' nests, but the bird isn't strong enough to break a nest open. So when a honey guide finds a bees' nest, it looks around for a ratel. A ratel will eat almost anything, but these animals are especially fond of honey.

The bird guides the ratel to the nest, hopping around and calling to lead it on. Then the ratel uses its strong claws and teeth to break the nest open. In this way both animals get what they want.

What if the honey guide can't find a ratel? Then it will lead another creature to the nest. African people often follow honey guides to find a free supply of honey.

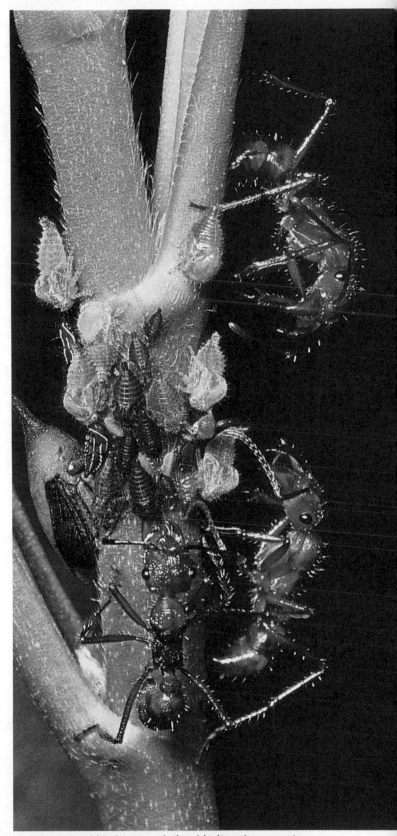

Ants and aphids have a relationship based on sweets. The ants protect the aphids so that they can get the sweet, sticky honeydew that the tiny insects secrete.

CALL IT A DAY!

Did you ever wonder why a week has seven days, or how the days got their names? The answers lie far back in history, in the times when people first developed calendars to keep track of the days as the year passed.

Many ancient calendars were very different from ours. The Chinese, for example, developed a calendar with sixty-day months and ten-day weeks. The Mayan Indians of Central America had thirteen-day weeks. But in ancient Mesopotamia, the Babylonians used a seven-day week. Their calendar was based on observations of the night sky, and they named each day for a different heavenly body. The ancient Hebrews also chose the seven-day week. For them, it mirrored the biblical story of creation, which says that the world was created in six days and that the seventh day was a day of rest.

The calendar of the Romans, who conquered much of the ancient world, originally had months but no weeks. But the Romans eventually adopted the seven-day week, and this custom gradually spread through their empire. The Romans named the days for the sun, the moon, and the gods that they associated with the five planets that can be seen with the naked eye.

Since our calendar is based on the Roman one, the seven-day week is still with us. There have been a few attempts to change it—during the French Revolution, for example, French authorities tried to switch to a ten-day week. But the change didn't take hold. And perhaps because the seven-day week is so old, each day has a tale of its own.

Sunday

In the Roman calendar, Sunday was *dies solis*—the day of the sun. As the Romans expanded their rule into Europe, they conquered tribes who spoke Germanic languages. These tribes adopted the Roman calendar, but they changed the names of the days to follow their own language. *Dies solis* became *Sunnandag* (sun's day). And over many years, that name developed into the modern English Sunday.

In the Christian tradition, Sunday is the Sabbath —a day of rest and worship. And as Christianity spread throughout the Roman Empire, the Romans changed the name of the first day of the week to *dies dominicus*, or day of the Lord. Thus languages that trace their roots to Latin, such as French and Spanish, have different names for Sunday: *dimanche* in French, *domingo* in Spanish.

Today Sunday is a day of relaxation in most places—schools and most businesses are closed, and people spend the day as they please. But in the past, observance of the Sabbath was often strictly enforced. The Puritan colonists who settled in New England, for example, had rigid rules: There could be no work and no play. People spent the day at the meeting house, praying and listening to sermons, and even simple activities such as cooking, running, kissing, and cutting hair were banned.

Monday

The Romans called the second day of the week *dies lunae*, or day of the moon. Modern languages that come from Latin have similar names—*lundi* in French, and *lunes* in Spanish. But the groups that spoke Germanic languages substituted their own word for the moon and came up with *Monandag*, which developed into the modern English Monday.

In ancient times, Monday was considered an unlucky day. This may have been because there were many superstitions about the moon. Some people even thought that gazing at the moon could drive a person insane. (In fact, the word "lunacy" comes from the Latin word for moon.) Monday was unpopular for another reason in days gone by. It was washday—and washing all a family's clothes by hand was a lot of work.

Even today, Monday is an unpopular day. This has less to do with superstition than with the fact that Monday marks the end of the weekend. After two days off, most people have to wake up early and head back to school or work. But some Mondays are better—in the United States and a number of other countries, many holidays fall on Mondays. And that gives everyone a three-day weekend.

Tuesday

The Romans named the third day of the week *dies Martis*, for Mars, the god of war. It is still known as *mardi* in French and as *martes* in Spanish. The Germanic people used the name of their own war god, Tiu—giving us the name Tuesday.

A few Tuesdays have special importance. The Tuesday after the first Monday in November is Election Day in the United States. People go to the polls to choose the officials who will run the government.

In the Christian calendar, Shrove Tuesday comes right before Lent, the 40-day period of prayer and fasting that leads up to Easter. It's the last chance for people to eat, drink, and make merry. In days gone by, people tried to use up all the butter and other fats they had on this day because they would have to give up fats during Lent. Rich, buttery foods became a Shrove Tuesday tradition. So this day is also known as Pancake Tuesday, and as Fat Tuesday (or *Mardi Gras*, in French).

Today some cities still hold Mardi Gras parades and festivals. The Mardi Gras celebration in New Orleans is one of the most famous. But most Tuesdays are just ordinary days. And Tuesdays of the past were pretty dull: Just as Monday was washday, Tuesday was ironing day.

Wednesday

The ancient Romans named the fourth day of the week after Mercury, the messenger of the gods and guardian of the spiritual life. Their *dies Mercurii* became *mercredi* in modern French and *miercoles* in Spanish.

The Germanic people chose a different god to honor on this day: Woden (or Odin), the chief of their gods and, like Mercury, the ruler of the spiritual life. In English, Woden's day became Wednesday—the name that's used today. But Wednesday goes by still another name in modern German: *Mittwoch*, or midweek. As the fourth of the seven days, Wednesday marks the midpoint of the week.

In some places, Wednesday was traditionally a market day. Farm families went to town to sell their produce and to buy the supplies they needed. Since they traveled by horse and wagon, the trip usually took all day.

Thursday

In ancient Rome, Jupiter (or Jove) was honored on *dies Jovis*, the fifth day of the week. Thus this day is called *jeudi* in French and *jueves* in Spanish. Jove was the Roman god of thunder and lightning, so Germanic tribes named the day after their own god of thunder—Thor. That gave us the modern English Thursday.

In Muslim countries, Thursday is the traditional day for weddings. Because Friday is the Muslim sabbath, everyone will have the day following the wedding off.

Friday

Venus, the goddess of love and beauty, was honored by the Romans on the sixth day of the week. Their *dies Veneris* became *vendredi* in French and *viernes* in Spanish. Germanic people chose another goddess: Frigga, the wife of Woden. That gave us Friday, the English name for this day.

In the past, Friday was considered an unlucky day. Perhaps this was because Friday was hang-

One of the most important U.S. holidays falls on the fourth Thursday in November: Thanksgiving. The first Thanksgiving feast was held by the Pilgrim settlers of New England in 1621. It lasted three days. After that, Thanksgiving gradually became a traditional way to celebrate the harvest. But every town chose its own day until 1863, when the feast was declared a national holiday.

In those days, a Thursday holiday was a welcome break from routine. Thursday was sweeping day in many homes. Furniture was dusted, floors were swept, and rugs were dragged outdoors and beaten to knock the dirt out. Before the days of vacuum cleaners, cleaning the house was a lot more work.

Saturday

The Romans named the last day of the week for Saturn, a god they associated with farming. And because the Germanic tribes had no god to substitute for Saturn, many of them kept the Roman name. Thus the Roman *dies Saturni* developed into the English name Saturday.

The French name *samedi* may also be a reference to the god of farming. It probably developed from *semer*, the French word for sowing. But the names used in some languages have a different origin. Saturday is the Jewish day of worship, and in the Bible the seventh day of the week is referred to simply as "sabbath." Thus Saturday is *sabado* in Spanish and *lordag* (Lord's day) in Swedish.

Traditionally, Saturday was bath day. Before homes had indoor plumbing, bath water had to be drawn from a well, carried indoors, and heated over a fire. Once a week was considered quite enough for this work, so every Saturday people cleaned up and got ready to begin a new week.

man's day—the day when public executions were held. And because the number thirteen was also considered unlucky, any Friday that was also the thirteenth day of the month was thought to be especially bad. Even today, some people are superstitious about Friday the Thirteenth.

For most people, however, Friday is one of the best days of the week. In Western countries, it's the last day of work and school—people look forward to the weekend. And in the Islamic religion, Friday is a day of worship. Thus schools, shops, and offices in Muslim countries are closed on this day.

A kaleidoscope is magical—it turns simple objects into images of fantastic beauty. And it's all done with mirrors. The mirrors—two of them—are inside the tube of the kaleidoscope, set up to form a V. Light reflected from objects at one end of the scope is bounced back and forth between them. When you look through the kaleidoscope's view hole, you see multiple images—the objects, their reflections in the mirrors, and reflections of the reflections.

The design in a kaleidoscope is always perfectly balanced, or symmetrical. In these designs, the most ordinary objects take on extraordinary beauty. Balloons, seashells, and flowers form delicate patterns. Common push pins explode in a colorful sunburst. And a bunch of items that might be found in your desk drawer—pencils, erasers, pennies, stamps—make up an intricate mosaic. Turning these common things into beautiful designs is the kaleidoscope's magic trick.

This 1837 painting shows the simple charm of folk art. Folk art is an appealing blend of art and craftsmanship, and it provides a fascinating record of days gone by.

THE CHARM OF FOLK ART

Works of art by great masters of the past are on display in museums all over the world. They are admired, studied, and analyzed by scholars. But art of quite another kind has become increasingly popular in recent years. This is folk art—painting, sculpture, and everyday decorated objects made by people who were self-taught and often knew little about formal artistic techniques or the works of great masters.

Folk art is a blend of art and craftsmanship. It appeals because of its freshness and simple charm, and it provides a fascinating record of life in the past. Today many museums have collections of folk art alongside their collections of formal art. And there are some museums devoted exclusively to it.

Throughout history, each culture has produced its own varieties of folk art. In America, the tradition of folk art began in colonial times and continued at least to the early 1900's. Some of the self-taught artists became well known. More often, their works were unsigned, and their names have been lost. But examples of their work remain.

PAINTING

Many American folk art painters—and they included children as well as adults—were amateurs who made pictures for their families and friends. Drawing and painting were popular hobbies, and many people assembled their works in sketchbooks.

There were also self-taught professionals, who used their skills to earn a living. Among the most common of these were portrait painters. Before photography became popular in the late 1800's, people were eager to have painters make portraits of family members. Thus many painters traveled from town to town, offering their services to people in each place they stopped.

Some of these paintings were quickly (and sometimes poorly) done. But many of the self-taught portrait painters showed high levels of skill and talent. The portraits generally followed a standard format. They showed people in stiff poses—seated or standing, often holding a book or some other object. Children were shown in these formal poses, too, holding their favorite toys or pets.

In most folk art portraits, the greatest attention was given to the face, to capture a likeness of the subject. The rest of the figure and the background often had a flat, simplified look. Still, the paintings provide a fascinating record of the clothes and furnishings of the past.

The large portraits painted by traveling artists were hung in the parlors of many homes, where visitors would see them. As a hobby, many people also made small watercolor portraits of friends and family members. Silhouettes cut from paper were another popular way of capturing a likeness.

Folk art painters also produced landscapes, seascapes, and other scenes. Seascapes generally showed famous ships or naval battles, while most landscapes were peaceful views of homes, farms, and towns.

Before the age of photography, people often asked artists to paint pictures of their homes for the same reason they had portraits painted—to record a likeness. Thus the main goal was to show the houses accurately. But the artists generally cleaned up the scene as they put it on canvas. Piles of junk, peeling paint, and other unattractive elements were left out, and everything was made to look neat and trim. These pictures show the homes of the past in an idealized way—as they might have been, not necessarily as they really were.

Historic events and scenes from the Bible were also favorite subjects for folk painters, both amateur and professional. So were still-life scenes, featuring flowers, fruit, and everyday objects. And in the 1800's another kind of painting became popular: the memorial. These works were made to mark the death of a family member. In somber tones, they generally showed family members gath-

Portraits of children, often shown holding something, were very popular in colonial times. While many were skillfully done, they showed the subjects in stiff poses.

Landscapes produced by folk artists showed peaceful views of homes, farms, and towns.

ered around the tombstone of the departed one—or perhaps draped across the stone, sobbing with grief.

Births, marriages, and other important life events were often recorded on documents that used a style of folk art called fraktur. A fraktur combined decorative lettering with elaborate and colorful watercolor designs—hearts, flowers, animals, and human figures. Fraktur birth and marriage certificates hung on the walls of many homes. Fraktur techniques were also used to illustrate Bible stories and other favorite legends and tales.

In many fraktur pieces, the writing is as pretty as the

design. In fact, before the days of typewriters and computers, penmanship was an art form. Schoolchildren were drilled in penmanship techniques, and there were even professional penmanship masters. People who had mastered those techniques often showed off their skills by creating gifts or presentation pieces for friends. In these works, the words take second place to the elaborate pictures and designs formed entirely by the free-flowing pen strokes.

SCULPTURE

Just like painting, folk art sculpture covers an enormous range. Artists used the materials that were at hand, such

30

as metal and pottery, to create their works. Aboard whaling ships, sailors whiled away the hours at sea by carving delicate designs

There were many kinds of folk art sculpture, but not all were designed with a specific use in mind. Many pieces were meant to simply delight the eye. This whirligig, or wind toy, sat on fences or posts outside many homes, its broad paddle-arms twirling in the breeze.

in the teeth and bones of whales, a technique called scrimshaw. Some of these pieces were purely decorative, but others were made for a specific purpose—perhaps kitchen utensils or yarn winders.

Many other folk art carvings were made of wood. And like the scrimshaw objects, many of these woodcarvings were designed to be used as well as admired. Among the most striking examples are the free-standing fig-

Births, baptisms, and other important life events were recorded on documents that used a style of folk art called fraktur—which combined decorative lettering with colorful and detailed watercolor designs.

ures that were used in the 1800's to advertise cigars. Large figures (some even life-size) were placed in front of tobacconists' shops or in shop windows; smaller ones were set on counter tops. They included a wide range of characters—Indians, soldiers, pot-bellied politicians, and Cuban and Turkish figures advertising cigars from those countries.

Other shopkeepers, from shoemakers to grocers, also used carved figures as advertisements. And carved poles with brightly painted stripes were used to mark barbershops, a tradition that began in England and spread to North America. In each case, the carvings made the shops easy to identify. They also reflected the skill and creativity of their makers.

Weathervanes also combined beauty with a purpose. They helped people predict the weather, since certain kinds of weather tend to come with winds from certain directions. But, perched on the rooftops of all sorts of buildings, weathervanes were also decorative sculpture. Some were carved from wood. But many were made from metal—silhouettes cut from sheets of tin, or molded shapes of copper or zinc.

The design of a weathervane often indicated the use of the building it adorned. There were fish vanes on fish markets, for example, while sheep and cows sat atop barns. But butterflies, eagles, Indians, and other fanciful designs were also used.

Later weathervanes were mass-produced from molds, but the early ones were made individually by hand. And before the days of factories and mass production, children's toys were also made by hand. Many were carved of wood. Animal figures, often set on wooden wheels, were especially popular. Relatively few of these hand-carved wooden toys survive today—evidence that they were loved and used by their owners.

Not all folk art sculpture was designed with a specific use in mind, however. Many pieces were meant simply to delight the eye. Figures of people and animals—dogs, cats, eagles, lions, and even some imaginary beasts—decorated many 19th-century rooms. Some were carved from pine and brightly painted. Others were ceramic, made by potters as gifts for family and friends. Many of these figures show their subjects in comical poses. Because of this, and because they had no use, these sculptures became known as "whimsies."

Somewhere between whimsies and toys were the whirligigs, or wind toys, that sat on posts or fences outside many homes in the 1800's. These were carved figures that, in place of arms, had broad paddles that twirled in the breeze. Often the whirligig makers chose military officers and policemen as subjects, poking fun at their serious expressions and stiff posture.

EVERYDAY ART

Some of the most interesting folk art includes the hundreds of hand-made everyday objects that filled homes in the 1700's and 1800's. Butter molds, pastry boards, and walking sticks all provided an outlet for the woodcarver's artistic expression. Pieces of furniture, especially chests and chairs, were carved and sometimes painted with colorful designs or with false woodgrain patterns. Geometric and floral patterns were stenciled on walls and worked into floor coverings.

Some of the most interesting pieces of folk art are the hand-made everyday objects that filled homes in the 1700's and 1800's. Pieces of furniture, for example, were often elaborately carved and colorfully painted.

Hand-made quilts are among the best-known examples of folk art in fabric. Many were exquisitely crafted in classic patterns of flowers and geometric shapes. Others featured unique designs from the quilt maker's imagination.

Potters produced decorated crocks and jugs in whimsical shapes. Tinsmiths made metal pots and boxes that were painted with bright floral designs. And designs were pierced into tin lanterns, so that the lanterns would cast patterned shadows.

Fabric provided another outlet for artistic expression. Decorative patterns were used to make everything from embroidered table covers to bed linens. Hand-made quilts are perhaps the best-known examples of folk art in fabric. Some were made in classic patterns of flowers and geometric shapes. Others featured unique designs dreamed up by the maker. And some were album quilts—designed and made by a group, with each person contributing a square to the design.

By the early 1900's, factories were mass producing most of the everyday objects that had once been made by hand. Mail-order catalogs and improved transportation made these manufactured items available even in remote rural areas. Meanwhile, ideas about art were being spread widely by newspapers and magazines. It became difficult for an individual artist *not* to be influenced by the latest trends and developments in the world of formal art.

Thus many people feel that true folk art died out in North America. But others think that the tradition lives on, and that folk art is being produced even today—by artists who are self-taught and steer their own creative course.

MILLION-DOLLAR DOLLS

On a foggy afternoon in London, Basil, the Great Mouse Detective, and Doctor David Q. Dawson were admiring a gift from Flaversham, the toymaker whom they had recently rescued from Professor Ratigan. Flaversham had sent Basil a wonderful invention that cleaned and refilled his pipe.

"It's rather clever, isn't it, Dawson?" said Basil as he watched the gadget work.

Suddenly they heard someone stomping up the stairs. "Get out of my way!" cried a woman's voice. "Boove, I say! Oadly the Great Bouse Detective cad help be!"

In burst a woman, waving a handkerchief and panting for breath. Behind her trotted Mrs. Judson, Basil's trusted housekeeper.

Before Mrs. Judson could stop her, the woman blew her nose and started talking. "Last night, someone broke into my house and stole my sapphires! The worst part is, the gems had been cut but they hadn't been

set into rings or necklaces yet. I'm sure the thief is selling them off at this very instant!"

The woman broke into sobs, and Basil waved impatiently at Dawson.

"There, there," said the doctor soothingly. "Calm yourself, Madame. Basil needs to ask some questions."

"I have all the information I need," said Basil, calmly picking up his pipe. "The woman before us is Countess Zenobia, who lives in a mansion on Hampstead Heath. She has an old Irish setter for a pet, and she leaves a back door open at night so the dog can go in and out of the house as he pleases. Last night a thief entered through that very door and stole the sapphires."

"I say!" exclaimed Doctor Dawson. "How did you figure all that out?"

"Elementary, my dear Dawson," stated Basil. "It's obvious that our guest has an elderly Irish setter—there are red and gray dog hairs on the hem of her velvet dress. Out of love for this animal, she no doubt gives it complete freedom of the house and yard. She also has the sniffles, which leads me to believe that she caught cold from leaving the back door open.''

The astonished woman blew her nose. Then she asked, ''But how did you guess my name?''

''That was more difficult,'' replied Basil. ''I noticed that you had the initial ''Z'' etched onto your locket, so I checked your ring finger to make sure that it didn't stand for your last name. You aren't married, so it must be your first name that begins with a Z. Fortunately, I read the newspaper this morning, and I saw a notice about a Zenobia, Countess of Kent, who had recently bought a mansion on Hampstead Heath.''

''That's all very well,'' sniffed the countess, ''but can you help me find my jewels?''

''I will try, Madame,'' answered Basil. ''Lead me to the scene of the crime.''

Basil and Doctor Dawson hopped into a cab and followed the countess's carriage to the mansion. As they entered, Basil asked, ''Madame, where did you keep the jewels?''

''In my dressing room, of course,'' she said. ''I'll show you.''

The countess and Dawson watched the Great Mouse Detective search every inch of the dressing room. ''Do you see anything?'' asked Dawson as Basil examined the rug with a magnifying glass.

''This is strange,'' said Basil, looking up. ''The countess's high heels have left marks on the rug, but there's no indication that someone else has stepped on it. It's almost as if the thief flew in!''

The detective stood up suddenly. When Doctor Dawson saw the horrified look on Basil's face, he cried, ''No! It can't be!''

''It can't be what?'' cried the countess.

''Fidget, Madame!'' replied Basil. ''An evil bat who works for an even more fiendish rat! Dawson and I thought we'd seen the last of those two.

''However,'' Basil added, ''we must check the backyard for clues before we reach any conclusions.''

"Why, yes," said Flaversham. "How did you guess?"

"May I see them?" requested Basil.

Puzzled, Flaversham hurried into the workshop and returned with a handful of glittering objects. "They're only made of glass," the toymaker said, "but they sparkle like jewels!"

"They really *are* jewels," announced Basil. "They are the sapphires that were stolen from the Countess of Kent's home last night. The question is, how did you get them?"

Flaversham quickly explained: "Someone came into my shop this morning with orders from . . ."

Dawson and the countess followed Basil into the yard. There the detective found a tiny mechanical ballerina in a pink dress.

"I say," fretted the doctor, "doesn't that look like Olivia Flaversham's doll?"

"Indeed it does," replied Basil. "We must hurry to Flaversham's toy shop. I fear for the safety of our friends!"

Leaving the countess behind, the Great Mouse Detective and his assistant sped across London to the toy shop. When Flaversham opened the door, he grinned. "Basil!" he cried. "I'm so happy to see you."

Without answering, the detective pushed his way into the room.

"Forgive my poor manners," remarked the detective, "but I had to make sure that you and Olivia were all right. Where is your daughter, by the way?"

"With a friend," Flaversham said. "Is something wrong?"

As Basil was about to explain, he noticed an object on the other side of the room. It was a porcelain-headed doll without any eyes. "Why doesn't that doll have eyes?" the detective asked.

"I haven't put them in yet," said Flaversham. "Why?"

Basil frowned and asked, "You weren't planning to put in blue eyes, were you?"

"Me!" came a voice from the door. They whirled around to see a familiar figure.

"Ratigan!" cried Basil. "I might have known!"

"Yes, it is I," sneered the professor. His henchmen surrounded Basil and the others.

Enraged, Flaversham shouted, "So it was you who asked me to make dolls for the poor children of Adzharia! I should have been suspicious when your man gave me those beautiful eyes!"

"Very ingenious, Ratigan," said Basil. "You smuggle the jewels out of the country in dolls. Isn't that rather tame for a master criminal?"

"Tame or not, Basil," chuckled Ratigan, "I don't plan to stop with measly little sapphires. My next target will be the Crown Jewels! I'll have no trouble stealing them— once you're out of the way!"

"You monster!" cried Dawson.

"You fool!" added Flaversham. Using all his might, the toymaker knocked over one of Ratigan's henchmen and ran for the door. When Ratigan lunged after him, Flaversham threw the sapphires in the professor's face.

In the commotion, Basil turned on another henchman and conked him on the head with his magnifying glass. Dawson tripped the third villain, and when the scoundrel lay sprawled on the floor, the doctor sat on him.

Seeing that his men had been overcome, Ratigan sprinted for the door before anyone could stop him. "I'll return!" promised Ratigan as he disappeared into the thick London fog. "You've not seen the last of me!"

In no time, Basil had contacted Scotland Yard to pick up Ratigan's lackeys. As for the Countess of Kent, she was very happy to see her sapphires again.

"Thank you so much!" she cried. "I promise never to leave my door open again, and I've decided what to do with the jewels. I'm going to have them set into a lovely collar for my dog!"

Basil nodded politely and bade the countess good-bye. He was eager to return home and begin devising a plan, a plan that would enable him to catch that rat of all rats, a professor named Ratigan!

THE GREAT SHAPE UP!

Keeping fit has been a craze for twenty years. Everywhere you go, you see people walking, running, jogging, and cycling to improve their health. Health clubs and exercise classes have opened up in almost every town. Books and magazines explain the benefits of fitness and the ways to achieve it.

Until recently, however, one group sat out this rush to become physically fit: kids. All through the 1970's and 1980's, as adults became fitter and fitter, young people became flabbier and flabbier. But now that's changing. As parents and teachers have become more aware of the benefits of exercise, they have begun to encourage kids to join in.

FIT FOR LIFE

Why are so many people exercising? The reason is simple: exercise can help you feel better and live longer. Studies have shown that regular exercise reduces the risk of heart disease and other serious illnesses, helps people lose weight, and boosts their self-esteem.

Exercise seems to lower levels of cholesterol, a substance in blood that's associated with heart disease. There's also evidence that people who exercise regularly handle stress better and are less likely to die from a variety of other causes. And you don't have to work out like Superman to get these

perform poorly in basic fitness tests. Many can't run a mile in thirteen minutes—a speed that many fitness experts suggest adults *walk* to promote fitness. More children are overweight today than were overweight twenty years ago. And many have high blood levels of cholesterol and other warning signs of heart disease.

Why haven't kids jumped on the fitness bandwagon? One reason is that young people are generally healthy. Heart disease and many of the other problems that exercise helps prevent don't usually develop until later in life, even if the warning signs are present early. Thus many young people feel little need to exercise.

On top of that, parents and teachers often wrongly assume that because young people appear to be active, they are getting all the exercise they need. Thus parents often don't encourage children to exercise, and many schools require only an hour or less of gym a week.

But the amount and kind of exercise you get in an hour of gym or an afternoon of play with your friends isn't really enough to make you physically fit. And there's strong evidence that people who begin to exercise when they are young are healthier throughout their lives. Re-

health benefits—even moderate exercise, such as a brisk daily walk, helps people live longer.

The link between fitness and health is so strong that U.S. corporations now spend about $300 million a year to encourage their employees to exercise. Some companies sponsor exercise classes; others have their own gyms, running tracks, and racquetball courts. They have found that these programs save money by reducing the cost of health care and ensuring that employees stay healthy and on the job.

While adults have been jogging and working out, however, kids have been busy at other activities—watching television and snacking. As a result, the majority of kids in the elementary through high school years

Vary your exercise program by including activities that are interesting and fun. Running, bicycling, and roller-blading all give your heart and lungs a good workout. So unglue yourself from the TV and shape up!

searchers have also discovered that fitness can have some immediate benefits for kids.

Some schools have found a link between fitness and academic performance. For example, a California school system began a program in which elementary-school students ran for twenty to forty minutes each morning. Teachers found that the children in the program did better on tests of basic academic skills. They also missed fewer school days because of illness.

A Canadian study compared students who had gym once a week to students who had gym every day and found similar results. The students who took gym daily spent less time in class but did better in reading and math. And other researchers think that being physically fit also makes children more confident socially.

All this has caused people to rethink the idea of fitness for young people. Many schools are now revising their physical education programs to include activities that promote overall fitness as well as teach sports skills. Some health clubs have begun to offer classes designed for kids, and there are even some clubs that are *just* for kids.

And parents are encouraging their children to join in when they exercise.

GET MOVING!

To turn a flabby body into a fit one—without injuring yourself in the process—you need both the right kind and the right amount of exercise.

The right kind of exercise consists of steady, sustained movement. This is known as aerobic exercise. "Aerobic" means "with oxygen." Muscles use oxygen when they work; the oxygen is taken in by your lungs and carried to the muscles by your blood. In aerobic exercise your heart and lungs work harder to supply the muscles with the oxygen they need. But the muscles' demand for oxygen never exceeds the ability of the heart and lungs to supply it.

The heart is made of muscle, and like any other muscle it grows stronger with use. That's why this type of exercise helps strengthen the heart and prevent heart disease. Aerobic exercise also improves general muscle tone, makes you more flexible, and burns up calories, helping to control your weight.

A second type of exercise consists of short bursts of very strenuous activity, such as sprinting or lifting heavy weights. In these anaerobic (without oxygen) exercises, the muscles use oxygen faster than the heart and lungs can supply it. (You can actually feel this happening—you feel pain or a burning sensation in the muscles.) Thus you can't continue the activity very long. Anaerobic exercise builds up individual muscles, but it won't promote general fitness or burn up calories the way aerobic exercise does.

Many health clubs have classes in aerobic exercise, aerobic dancing (exercise done to music), and similar activities. But the really great thing about aerobic exercise is that there are many different ways to do it. Running, jogging, bicycling, swimming, rowing, and even roller skating all can give your heart and lungs a good workout. So can sports such as basketball, cross-country skiing, tennis, and racquetball.

This means that you can vary your exercise program and include a range of activities that are interesting and fun. If you do this, you'll be less likely to become a "fitness drop-out" and give up your workouts.

This approach is called cross-training, and it has another benefit: Varying your activities allows you to focus on different aspects of fitness. Aerobic dancing is great for increasing flexibility and coordination, for example. Rowing helps build upper-body strength, while swimming and cross-country skiing give all your muscles a workout.

The key in all these activities is to work hard enough to make your heart beat faster, but not so hard that you get really out of breath and your muscles start to hurt. To get the full benefit of aerobic exercise, you also have to keep the activity up for a period of time.

How long and how often you exercise depend a lot on how fit you are to begin with and how strenuous the activity you choose is. Fifteen or twenty minutes of brisk walking, three or four times a week, may be enough for someone who's badly out of shape. As your fitness improves, you can gradually lengthen your workouts and add more strenuous activities, such as running or jogging.

Whatever your fitness level, experts suggest taking some precautions to avoid injuries when you exercise:

• Begin your workout by warming up— doing easy activities that get the blood flowing to your muscles. Many people believe that stretching exercises are good warm-up activities. Or, if you're going to jog or run, you might start by walking briskly for three to five minutes.

• Finish your workout with a few minutes of easy activity, too—if you run, walk for a few minutes when you're done. As you walk, the action of your muscles helps push blood back to the heart, keeping your circulation flowing smoothly as your heart rate gradually returns to normal.

• Don't push yourself too hard when you exercise—do what's comfortable for you. Always increase your workload gradually, to give your muscles a chance to build strength for the increased work. And anytime you feel pain, stop what you're doing.

• Many experts add that children under 15 should avoid certain very strenuous activities, such as long-distance running. The reason is that their bones aren't fully developed and may be damaged by too much stress.

As long as you keep these precautions in mind, exercise can only do you good. So what are you waiting for? It's time to get off the couch, stop snacking, and shape up!

WHAT AM I?

Here's an animal you're not likely to see —even if you travel to every zoo in the world! This peculiar-looking mystery creature has fur, feathers, scales, a tough hide, claws, and hooves, all at the same time. It has a big hump and two different pairs of wings on its back. Its four legs don't match, and its tail is enormous. And it has floppy ears, branching antlers, big eyes that bug out on top of its head, and a *very* strange nose.

All the same, when you begin to examine this curious creature more closely, it may look familiar—or, at least, parts of it will. Surely you've seen that hump somewhere before . . . and that funny-looking tongue must remind you of something. In fact, this odd creature is made up of parts of other animals, some of them exotic and some quite common. It could be the creation of a mad scientist—but it has really been put together as a game for you.

Can you identify the thirteen different animals that were used to make this mystery creature? Find each of the numbered parts, and see if you can guess what animal it comes from. (The answers are given below.)

Iraq invaded Kuwait in 1990, and several hundred thousand U.S. troops found themselves in an unlikely place—in the desert protecting Saudi Arabian oilfields.

THE PERSIAN GULF CRISIS

The largest U.S. military force to operate overseas since the Vietnam War stood poised for action in the Persian Gulf region at the end of 1990. The force, some 400,000 strong and joined by troops from other countries, was sent after Iraq invaded the tiny Persian Gulf nation of Kuwait in August.

The Iraqi invasion of Kuwait sparked an outcry around the world. Iraq, one of the strongest military powers in the Middle East, acted with brutal disregard for the rights of its small neighbor. Moreover, seizing Kuwait gave Iraq control of 20 percent of the world's known oil reserves and put its troops in a position to threaten the even richer reserves of Saudi Arabia.

THE INVASION

Under dictator Saddam Hussein, Iraq had grown into a major Middle East power. From 1980 to 1988, it had fought a war with Iran, its neighbor to the east. The war had ended in a stalemate. But it left Iraq with a battle-hardened army of about a million soldiers—the largest in the Arab world—and some highly advanced weapons systems, including missiles and chemical weapons. Sad-

dam Hussein continued to build up his forces after the war, and it was rumored that he was developing nuclear weapons.

The invasion of Kuwait grew out of a dispute over oil and territory. Iraq was an oil-exporting country with substantial reserves. But the war with Iran had battered its economy and left it with debts of $80 billion, much of which had been lent by Saudi Arabia and Kuwait. A drop in oil prices made the situation more difficult by reducing Iraq's income from oil.

Saddam Hussein accused Kuwait and some other members of the Organization of Petroleum Exporting Countries (OPEC) of pumping too much oil, thus driving down the price. He also said that Kuwait was drawing more than its share from a vast oil field that lies beneath both countries. He demanded payments and debt relief totaling about $44 billion. And he revived an old boundary dispute, demanding control over territory that would give his country greater access to the Persian Gulf. When Kuwait didn't immediately agree to his demands, Iraqi forces invaded on August 2.

The Iraqi troops had no difficulty overcoming the far smaller Kuwaiti forces. The Kuwaiti ruling family fled the country. (Kuwait, an emirate, had been ruled by the same family for about 250 years. The emir at the time of the invasion was Sheik Jabir al-Ahmad al-Sabah.) The Iraqi forces then moved south and massed on Kuwait's border with Saudi Arabia.

The invasion was immediately condemned by countries around the world. The United Nations demanded that Iraq withdraw from Kuwait and voted to impose a stiff trade embargo and other economic sanctions against Iraq. And within days of the attack, the United States sent its first ground forces and warplanes to Saudi Arabia, to block a possible Iraqi invasion of that country.

The United States also sent Navy ships to the Persian Gulf region and announced that it would back up the U.N. embargo by imposing a blockade on Iraqi ports. Ships would be prevented, by force if necessary, from carrying goods in and out of Iraqi ports.

But Iraq didn't back down. Instead, it increased its troops in Kuwait and announced that it had annexed the country, making Kuwait a province of Iraq. Iraqi forces reportedly assaulted and killed Kuwaiti citizens and looted the country, even taking equipment from hospitals. Many Kuwaitis were forced from their homes, and eventually as much as half Kuwait's population fled the country. So did thousands of foreigners, many of them workers from Egypt, India, and other countries. Most made their way to emergency camps set up along the Iraq-Jordan border, where they waited in squalid conditions for transportation home.

Meanwhile, Iraq demanded that foreign embassies in Kuwait close. Those that refused, including the U.S. embassy, were surrounded, and supplies of food, water, and electricity were cut off. And thousands of people from other countries, especially Westerners, were rounded up and taken hostage by the Iraqis. Many were taken to important military and industrial sites in Iraq. The Iraqis hoped to prevent attacks on these sites by placing hostages there as "human shields."

THE BUILDUP

The world reaction to the invasion represented a rare show of unity. For one of the few times in recent history, the United States and the Soviet Union stood together in condemning Iraq. And the U.S. troops and ships were soon joined by forces from other countries.

In the Arab world, however, Iraq's action produced a division. Saudi Arabia, Egypt, and other moderate Arab countries condemned the invasion. So did Syria, Iraq's western neighbor and its major rival. These countries sent troops to Saudi Arabia or supported the growing international force there in other ways.

But Saddam Hussein won the admiration of many Arabs by presenting himself as a champion of the poor against oil-rich states like Kuwait. To some, he seemed the only Arab leader able to stand up to the West. He also tried to broaden the issue, claiming that the question of Kuwait couldn't be settled unless other Middle East questions, such as Israel's occupation of territory claimed by Palestinian Arabs, were settled at the same time. Although he had never been a religious leader, he called on Muslims to rise up in a holy war against foreigners and "corrupt" Arab states.

American troops often trained in gas masks because of the possibility that Iraq might use its chemical weapons.

ARAB COUNTRIES OF THE MIDDLE EAST

The Arabs of the Middle East have much in common. Most, for example, are Muslims. But when Iraq invaded Kuwait, a split was created in the Arab world. Arab countries took different stands on the invasion, reflecting their individual views and circumstances.

Egypt. A major Middle East power, Egypt has often rivaled Iraq for influence in the region. It opposed the invasion and sent troops to defend Saudi Arabia from possible Iraqi attack. Egypt is a relatively poor country, and it receives about $2 billion a year in U.S. aid. A parliamentary republic led by President Hosni Mubarak, it is the only Arab country to recognize Israel.

Lebanon. Since the 1970's, Lebanon has been decimated by civil war between Christian and Muslim factions. This strife continued in 1990. The Lebanese government, which is dominated by Syria, opposed the Iraqi invasion and supported the countries that sent troops to Saudi Arabia's defense.

Syria. Under the firm control of dictator Hafez al-Assad, Syria has long been one of Iraq's most powerful rivals in the Middle East. It condemned the invasion of Kuwait and sent troops to aid Saudi Arabia. The Syrian government is known for its ruthless suppression of dissent and has been accused of aiding terrorists in attacks on the West. The country has some oil reserves, but it isn't a major oil producer.

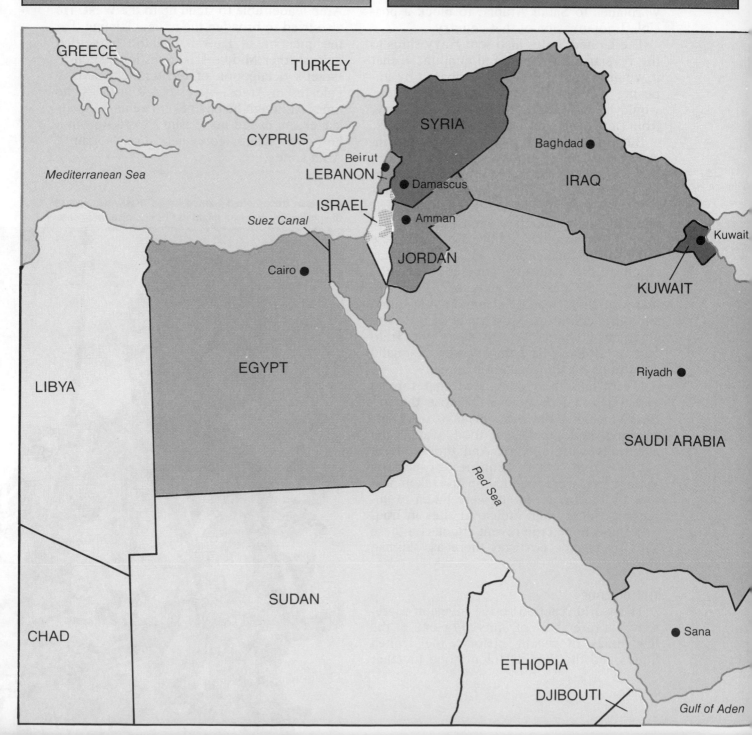

Jordan. A trading partner of Iraq, Jordan was caught in the middle of the crisis. Its ruler, King Hussein, agreed to abide by U.N. sanctions against Iraq but opposed military action and tried to act as a mediator. The sanctions hurt Jordan's economy, and the country was burdened by thousands of people fleeing from Iraq and Kuwait.

Saudi Arabia. A monarchy led by King Fahd of the Saud family, Saudi Arabia has vast oil reserves and was directly threatened by the invasion. Although it had distanced itself from the West in the past, it permitted a huge buildup of Western military forces on its soil and agreed to help pay for the force. The government requires strict observance of Islamic customs; women, for example, go veiled in public and are barred from many activities.

Iraq. Under dictator Saddam Hussein, Iraq was seeking to become the dominant power in the region. In the 1980's, during a long war with neighboring Iran, it built up a huge army and advanced weapons systems. The government was known for brutal repression and had even used chemical weapons against a group of its own citizens, the Kurds. Although Iraq has huge oil reserves, its economy is weak and most Iraqis are poor. Saddam Hussein was seen by some Arabs as a champion of the poor against the oil-rich Arab states.

Kuwait. A small country with vast oil reserves, Kuwait was ruled by the al-Sabah family from the mid-1700's until Iraq's 1990 invasion. Kuwait had supported Iraq in its war with Iran; but when that conflict ended in 1988, Kuwait became involved in a dispute with Iraq over oil reserves and territory.

Bahrain. A small Persian Gulf state with minor oil reserves, Bahrain condemned the Iraqi invasion. This country, an emirate with a hereditary ruler, is the site of an important U.S. naval base. After the invasion, it permitted U.S. and British combat aircraft to be stationed on its soil.

Qatar. Another oil-producing Persian Gulf emirate, Qatar took a firm stand against Iraq and, like Bahrain, permitted the deployment of Western warplanes within its borders. The country is known for its strict observance of Islamic customs.

United Arab Emirates. A group of seven small city-states governed by hereditary rulers, the United Arab Emirates has huge oil reserves. It, too, condemned Iraq and allowed the United States to deploy warplanes in its territory. One of the wealthiest Arab states, it also agreed to help pay for the multi-national force formed to opposed Iraq.

Oman. Oman, which has long had close relations with Britain, was firmly against the Iraqi invasion and also accepted the deployment of U.S. and British combat planes. Oman exports oil, but its reserves aren't as large as those of some other countries in the region.

Yemen. In May, 1990, North Yemen (which had ties with the West) merged with South Yemen (a Marxist state) to form a single country. A relatively poor country with some oil reserves, Yemen leaned toward Iraq in the crisis but said that it would observe the U.N. sanctions. Relations with Saudi Arabia were strained when the Saudis expelled hundreds of Yemenis who were working there.

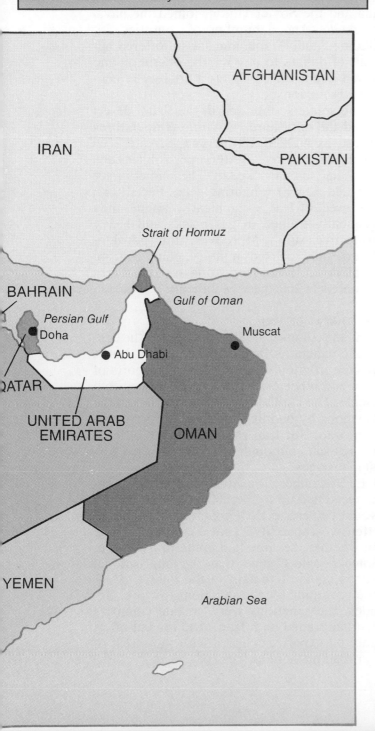

Thus Libya, Jordan, the Palestine Liberation Organization (PLO), and several of the poorer Arab countries didn't condemn the invasion. They called for Arab leaders to meet and work out a compromise. But these efforts were unsuccessful—Iraq refused to give up its claims on Kuwait, while Kuwait and its allies firmly refused to give up territory or grant other concessions as a result of Iraq's aggression.

As weeks stretched into months, both sides built up their forces. Iraq signed a peace treaty with Iran, which allowed it to move troops away from its eastern border and station them in the south. They dug into defensive positions along the Kuwait-Saudi border.

By late October, the United States had sent more than 200,000 troops to take part in the operation, known as Desert Shield. Most were stationed in the Saudi desert. They included reserve units that were called up for the crisis, as well as full-time soldiers. Among them were substantial numbers of women, who were barred from combat but

When Iraq seized its wealthy neighbor Kuwait, it gained control of 20 percent of the world's known oil reserves.

filled many support roles. The sight of female soldiers in fatigues was new to many Saudis. In Saudi Arabia's Islamic culture, women are heavily veiled and are forbidden to drive cars and perform many kinds of work.

The U.S. forces were joined by about 60,000 Saudi troops and smaller numbers from France, Britain, Kuwait and the other Persian Gulf states, Syria, Egypt, Pakistan, Bangladesh, and Morocco. Argentina sent a token force, and Czechoslovakia sent a small unit skilled in defense against chemical weapons. In addition, 95,000 Turkish troops were massed on Iraq's northern border. More than a dozen countries, including Canada and the Soviet Union, joined the naval blockade. And a number of countries, including Saudi Arabia and Japan, offered billions of dollars to pay for the operation and to aid countries that were hurt by the economic sanctions.

The soldiers stationed in the Saudi desert found the duty hard. Daytime temperatures soared as high as 120°F (49°C). Water—as much as 6 gallons (23 liters) per soldier each day—had to be trucked in. The soldiers were weighed down by fighting gear. Faced with the threat of Iraq's chemical weapons, they frequently trained in gas masks and heavy protective suits. Moreover, the powdery desert sand caused military equipment to break down. Even navigating in the flat, monotonous landscape was difficult.

THE THREAT OF WAR

As the troops waited in the desert, the economic sanctions began to take hold. Iraq's income from oil was cut off, and imports of food and other essentials were reduced to a trickle. The United Nations strengthened the sanctions by banning most air traffic to and from Iraq. But Iraq showed no sign of leaving Kuwait, although it released some foreign hostages.

In November, President George Bush announced that up to 200,000 more U.S. troops would be sent to the Gulf, to give the force offensive capability. That sparked a debate on whether the time had come to use force. Some people argued that the international troops couldn't remain in the desert indefinitely, waiting for the sanctions to work. Besides, the sanctions were hurting countries that had traded with Iraq. And the cut-off of Iraqi oil exports, coupled with the threat of war, had made oil prices soar.

SADDAM: A BRUTAL DICTATOR

By invading Kuwait, Saddam Hussein seemed to be making a bid to dominate the Arab world. But the 53-year-old Iraqi president (who is commonly referred to by his first name) had already gained a reputation as a brutal and ambitious dictator.

Born in 1937 to a peasant family, Saddam was orphaned at an early age and was raised by an uncle. As a young man, he joined the Baath Party, a political group that supports Arab nationalism. He was among a group of party members who tried to assassinate Iraqi dictator Abdel Karim Kassem in 1959. The plot failed, and he fled to Egypt. But when the Baath Party seized power in a coup in 1968, he returned and became the second most powerful person in the government. Eleven years later, he became president.

Saddam brought stability to Iraq through severe repression. He eliminated political opponents; simply criticizing his rule could bring death. He also built up Iraq's military strength, developing missiles and chemical weapons. In 1981, Israel bombed and destroyed an Iraqi nuclear reactor that it said was being used to develop nuclear weapons. Saddam used chemical weapons in his eight-year war with Iran and to put down unrest among a group of his own citizens, the Kurds.

Having eliminated his critics, Saddam was said to be isolated and to lack a clear picture of the strength of world opposition to his invasion of Kuwait. There was talk that Iraqi army officers who saw the situation more clearly might overthrow him, to prevent a war that Iraq would likely lose. But after years of repression, there was no organized Iraqi opposition. And Saddam had already survived several assassination attempts.

Murals of Saddam Hussein appear throughout Iraq.

Others argued that the sanctions should be given more time and that military action, if it proved necessary, should be directed by the United Nations. There was debate, too, about the U.S. goals. The United States said that it was in the Gulf region to restore the Kuwaiti government and establish peace and security. But it wasn't clear if establishing peace and security meant overthrowing Saddam. And keeping Mideast oil in friendly hands seemed to be another goal.

In late November, the United Nations set a deadline for Iraq's withdrawal from Kuwait: January 15, 1991. After that, U.N. members would be free to use any means, even force, to drive Iraq out. Soon after, Iraq released its remaining foreign hostages, including about 800 Americans. At the same time, however, Iraq continued to build up its troops. There was a last-ditch effort to arrange high-level talks between Iraq and the United States, but the two sides couldn't agree on dates for the talks. Thus fears of war remained strong.

One thing was clear: If war came, thousands of people would be killed. Yet to let Iraq's invasion stand would be to turn aside as a brutal aggressor destroyed an independent country and reached for a stranglehold on the region's vital oil supplies.

GO FLY A KITE

Some people call it "painting the sky." Others say it's "dancing with the wind." But most people call it just plain "kite flying."

Today, millions of people all around the world are painting the sky with colorful kites. Kite flying is fun, and it's easy to do. Look up on a breezy spring afternoon and you're bound to see at least one diamond-shaped kite—probably the most familiar kite shape in North America. But you're also likely to see kites shaped like butterflies, eagles, flags, airplanes, flowers, masks—almost anything imaginable. For in recent years, the art of creating kites has become as popular as the sport of flying them.

MORE THAN AMUSEMENT

No one knows for sure who made the first kites, but it's believed that they were invented in China more than 2,000 years ago. According to one legend, a farmer got the idea when a gust of wind blew off his hat. The hat had a string that tied under the farmer's chin, so he didn't lose it. But the ability of the wind to carry his hat gave him an idea for a toy with which to amuse himself and his friends.

From early times, however, kites have been more than toys. They have had many practical uses. Some uses were military. About 500 A.D. one Chinese emperor used kites to signal his soldiers. The soldiers would work on nearby farms until they saw the kites flying above the emperor's palace. This was a signal that they should rush to the palace to help defend it against enemies seen approaching on the horizon.

During the American Civil War in the 1860's, the Union used kites to scatter leaflets over Confederate troops. The leaflets urged the Confederates to surrender, promising them amnesty if they would lay down their arms. During the Boer War in South Africa in the late 1890's, large kites were used to carry British soldiers over the fighting front to observe the enemy. During World Wars I and II, kites were used to disable enemy aircraft.

Kites have also been valuable scientific tools. The most famous experiment involving a kite was conducted by Benjamin Franklin during a thunderstorm in 1752. Flying a kite made of a silk handkerchief stretched on two cedar sticks, Franklin proved that lightning was the same as the electric current that flows through wires. (This was a very dangerous experiment; it could easily have killed Franklin!)

From the 1700's until the early 1900's, kites were used to collect weather data. Thermometers, anemometers, and other instruments used to measure weather factors were attached to kites and launched into the sky. Kites have also been used to tow boats and sleds and carry cameras into the atmosphere to take pictures of the Earth.

And kites are used to celebrate special occasions. In Japan, for example, people fly kites to welcome in the new year and to celebrate Children's Day on May 5. In China, the Festival of Ascending on High is actually a celebration of the practice of kite flying.

AN EXHILARATING PASTIME

Today most people fly kites simply for fun. Kites come in a wide variety of shapes, materials, and colors. There are diamonds, dragons, centipedes, birds, windsocks, and boxes. They're made of paper, plastic, nylon, satin. And they come in every color of the rainbow—usually, the more brilliant, the better.

Many kites are painted with fantastic designs. Some have appliquéd designs, with the part under the appliqué cut away so that all parts are equally filled with light. Still other kites are made of patchwork, with designs taken from classic quilt patterns. The result is often an item of great beauty. Many kites are so beautiful that people use them to decorate walls in their homes.

Despite the variety, all kites have three basic parts. The **wing surface** is designed to be lifted by the wind. The **flying line** is used to control the flight of the kite and keep it from being blown away. The **bridle** is the means by which the flying line is connected to the kite. It holds the face of the kite at an angle to the wind.

Traditional kites are flat and rigid. They usually need a tail to help keep the bottom of the kite down and the nose tilted up.

KITING TIPS

To have a truly unique kite, make and decorate your own! Kite-building materials are inexpensive and easy to obtain. Just choose the lightest materials possible: The heavier the material, the more it will pull the kite down.

The wing can be made from paper, cloth, nylon, or plastic. If you use paper, avoid the kinds that easily tear or crease. If you prefer cloth, select a fabric such as cotton sailcloth, which is lightweight yet tightly woven.

The wing's supporting frame is made of wood. Use wood that's light, strong, and flexible. Craft shops sell special kite dowels, but you can also use pieces of bamboo, spruce, or white pine.

Buy strong string for the flying line. You might consider using linen cord, fishing line, or braided nylon twine. The bridle may be made from ordinary string or a thin cord.

A word of caution: never use metal in any part of your kite. Don't use metal frames, metal-coated materials, wire, or tinsel. Metal conducts electricity, and you could get a shock.

Many books give directions for making various kite shapes. Start with something basic. The more elaborate the kite, the more complex the construction. But even a simple diamond-shaped kite can look spectacular. Choose colorful fabrics. Paint or appliqué wild designs on the wing.

Whatever kind of kite you build, keep in mind that for a kite to stay in the air it should be symmetrical—each side should be similar to the other.

Once you have your kite, you're ready to fly! Here are tips to help make your kite dance in the wind.

• Don't run with a kite to launch it. Stand with your back to the wind. Have a friend stand about 100 feet (30 meters) away, holding the kite pointing upward. As your friend lets go of the kite, pull in the line with a hand-over-hand motion. The kite will rise in the air.

• Pulling in on the kite line makes a kite rise. Letting the line out allows the wind to carry the kite away, but at the same time causes the kite to lose altitude. Combining the two—pulling, letting out line, and pulling again in a kind of pumping action—lets your kite fly high and far.

• Pulling on the line makes a kite move in the direction it is already headed. If your kite is diving or is otherwise out of control, don't pull. It only makes matters worse. Let your line go completely slack. When the kite rights itself, pull in on the line to make it rise into the air again.

M. McLean

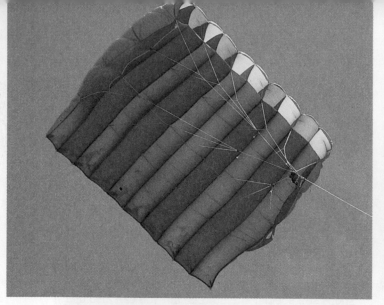

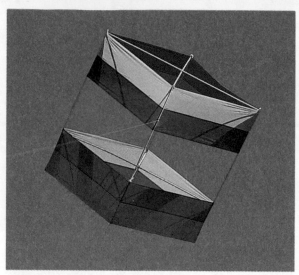

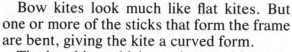

Bow kites look much like flat kites. But one or more of the sticks that form the frame are bent, giving the kite a curved form.

The box kite, which was invented in 1893, is a rigid kite consisting of two or more open-ended boxes. The boxes may be square, oblong, or triangular. Large box kites are powerful flyers. Those 6 feet (2 meters) or longer generally require two people to hold and maneuver the flying line.

The first nonrigid kite was the parawing, designed in the 1940's. (Hang-gliders are an adaptation of the parawing.) Sometimes called the flexiwing, the parawing has no central spine or other supporting sticks.

Another big step came in the 1960's, when a huge kite called the parafoil was designed. The parafoil resembles a parachute and has incredible lifting and gliding power. It's made entirely of fabric, with no supporting sticks.

Then there are the amazing kites from Asia: The caterpillar kite consists of a series of disks connected by lengths of string. The snake kite has a long tapering tail that ripples in the breeze. The butterfly kite, which flies best in light winds, has bowed wings. The Chinese lantern kite looks like a giant tube or can that is open at both ends.

Typically, a kite has a single flying line. If you add a second line, you can try stunt flying—creating loops, circles, hairpin turns, and other maneuvers. Expert fliers can even make their kites do somersaults and dance to music. And for even tighter control, some people use four flying lines, called quad lines.

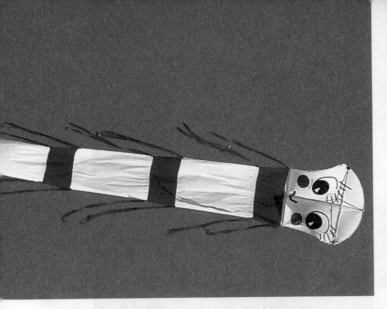

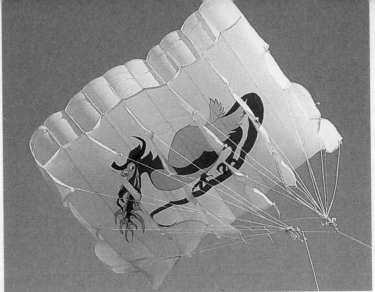

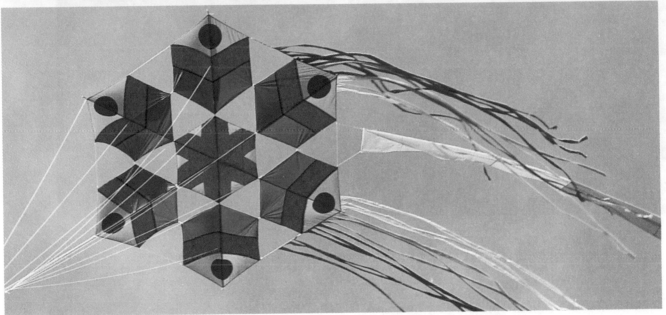

The largest kite ever built had an area of 6,000 square feet (557 square meters). When it was sent aloft, seventy people held onto it. But it was so powerful that it almost pulled those seventy people into the sky.

What is believed to have been the longest kite was called the Thai Snake. When fully stretched out across the sky, it had a length of almost half a mile (0.8 kilometer).

SHARING THE FUN

Sometimes it's fun to be all alone as you fly your kite. But at other times you may want to share your pleasure—perhaps with a few friends or perhaps with thousands of other kiting enthusiasts. One of the most popular group events is the annual Kite Festival, which takes place at the Smithsonian Institution in Washington, D.C. Participants can fly any kite they want. But if you wish to enter any of the festival contests, you must fly a homemade kite that is able to reach an altitude of 100 feet (33 meters) for a least one minute.

This is only one of the hundreds of kite festivals held in cities and towns in many countries. People compete for prizes, exchange kite-building secrets, and have a great time. Even those who don't fly kites enjoy these colorful events. Many people who come "just to watch" return the following year with kites of their own, for they have learned the joys of this fascinating pastime.

JENNY TESAR
Series Consultant
Wonders of Wildlife

HUMMINGBIRDS: LITTLE FLYING JEWELS

In a burst of brilliant color, a tiny bird appears. It hovers for a second in front of a flower, its wings beating so fast that they are nothing but a blur. Then it zips away, vanishing as quickly as it appeared.

The bird could only be a hummingbird, one of nature's smallest and most charming creatures. Hummingbirds invite superlatives. Besides including the world's smallest birds, they are among the most colorful, with iridescent feathers in a range of jewel-like tones. They are easily the most acrobatic birds, performing astounding feats in flight. And without doubt, hummingbirds are among the most fascinating of all birds.

THE LONG AND THE SHORT OF IT

There are more than 300 different kinds, or species, of hummingbirds. All of them live only in the Western Hemisphere, but they are found in almost all parts of it.

The smallest hummingbird—and the smallest bird—is the rare and tiny bee hummingbird of Cuba. This bird really could be mistaken for a bee. It weighs about as much as a penny and is just 2½ inches (6.4 centimeters) long. And half that length is made up of its beak and its tail!

The largest hummingbird is the giant hummingbird, which lives in western South America from Ecuador to Chile. It weighs ten times as much as the bee hummingbird and is over 8 inches (21 centimeters) long, about the length of a common starling.

In between the bee and the giant are hummingbirds of all sorts and sizes. But most of the birds are small. And while not all hummingbirds are colorful, many are famous for their vivid tones—green, blue, ruby, violet, magenta. The brilliance of the birds' feathers has led people to call them "flying jewels."

This brilliance occurs because the feathers

of many hummingbirds are iridescent, so that they catch and reflect light. When sunlight strikes a hummingbird's feathers at the right angle, the color seems to explode in a burst of fiery glitter. Depending on where you stand and how the light strikes the bird, it may seem that there are several colors where in fact there is only one. When no light shines on the feathers, they appear black.

Males are often more colorful than females, although this isn't always so. In many species the colors are concentrated on the bird's crown or throat. Some hummingbirds also have special adornments—elaborate crests or long, streaming tail feathers—that add to their beauty. The streamertail, found in Jamaica, has a forked tail more than 6 inches (15 centimeters) long, far longer than its body.

Hummingbirds share certain other features. Most hummingbirds have long, slender bills that are ideal for sipping the birds' favorite food—the nectar of flowers. A hummingbird inserts its bill deep into a flower and then extends its long tongue to lap up the sugary nectar.

In South America, where there are many kinds of hummingbirds, scientists have noticed that each type has a bill of a certain length. The shortest are those of hummingbirds called thornbills and are just half an inch (1.25 centimeters) long. The longest bills are those of the swordbills—at five inches (over 12 centimeters), they are almost as long as the birds themselves.

In addition, some birds have straight bills, and some have curved bills. Each bill is ideal for feeding on the nectar of certain types of flowers. This allows many kinds of hummingbirds to live in the same area without competing for the same food sources.

TINY ACROBATS

Besides their tiny size and vivid colors, the most remarkable feature of hummingbirds is their ability to perform incredible feats in flight. A hummingbird will hover motionless in front of a flower to sip nectar and then actually fly backward to withdraw its bill from the bloom. It will dart a few inches to the side and hover again, perfectly positioned to sip from the next flower. Then it will suddenly dart away, reaching speeds of

Hummingbirds build their tiny nests of plant fibers, moss, and spider silk, and the nests can easily fit in a link of chain. Some of the brilliantly colored birds are so small, they can sit atop the eraser of a pencil.

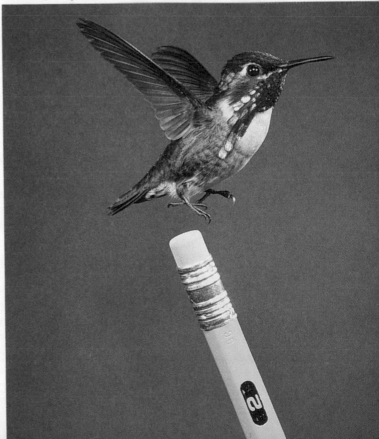

30 miles (48 kilometers) an hour almost immediately. Hummingbirds can even fly *upside down* for short distances. They are the only birds that can perform all these acrobatic feats.

Hummingbirds are such accomplished aerialists that they use their wings for everything—in fact, most appear unable to hop or walk. Mother hummingbirds have even been seen to shift position on their nests by rising on their wings, turning in the air, and settling down again like little helicopters.

A hummingbird's wings beat so fast—50 times a second in some species, as much as 80 times in others—that they are just blurs to the eye. (The rapid beating creates a humming sound, which has given the birds their name.) But by using slow-motion photography and by studying the way the birds' wings are put together, scientists have learned a lot about these incredible stunt flyers.

When the tiny birds hover, for

example, their wings trace a figure-eight pattern in the air, moving forward and backward instead of up and down. The wings pivot so that each forward stroke and each backward stroke gives lift, helping the bird stay in the air. But the strokes cancel each other out, so the bird stays motionless.

HUMMINGBIRD HABITS

Most hummingbirds live in South America near the equator, where the climate is warm all year. But hummingbirds are found in almost all parts of the Western Hemisphere. The ruby-throated hummingbird breeds in much of the eastern United States and Canada but winters in Central America. The rufous hummingbird is found as far north as Alaska in the summer; it spends winters in Mexico. Other hummingbird species are found in the Caribbean and as far south as the tip of South America.

Even hummingbirds that don't migrate with the changing seasons travel over a wide area, constantly searching for food. For its size, a tiny hummingbird requires astounding amounts of food. It must consume half its

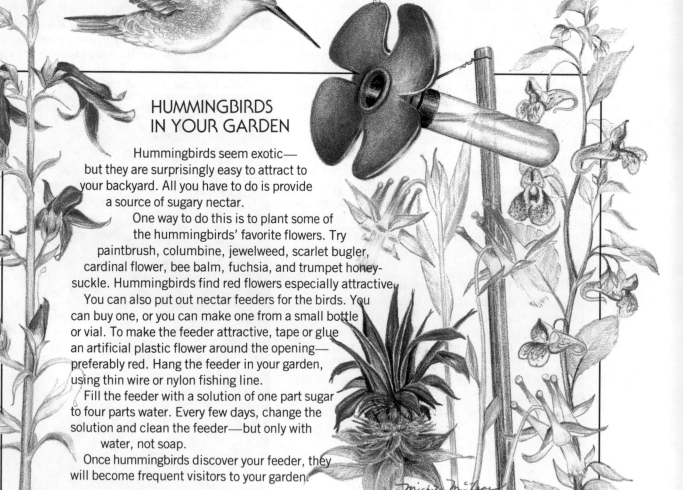

HUMMINGBIRDS IN YOUR GARDEN

Hummingbirds seem exotic—but they are surprisingly easy to attract to your backyard. All you have to do is provide a source of sugary nectar.

One way to do this is to plant some of the hummingbirds' favorite flowers. Try paintbrush, columbine, jewelweed, scarlet bugler, cardinal flower, bee balm, fuchsia, and trumpet honeysuckle. Hummingbirds find red flowers especially attractive.

You can also put out nectar feeders for the birds. You can buy one, or you can make one from a small bottle or vial. To make the feeder attractive, tape or glue an artificial plastic flower around the opening—preferably red. Hang the feeder in your garden, using thin wire or nylon fishing line.

Fill the feeder with a solution of one part sugar to four parts water. Every few days, change the solution and clean the feeder—but only with water, not soap.

Once hummingbirds discover your feeder, they will become frequent visitors to your garden.

body weight in food each day—the equivalent of a full-grown man eating 300 hamburgers. To get what they need, hummingbirds feed throughout the day and often into dusk, when other birds have roosted for the night.

It was once thought that the birds lived entirely on flower nectar, but this isn't so. The sugary nectar provides a source of quick energy. That's essential for these active little birds, which burn up more energy than any other warm-blooded creature. But hummingbirds also need protein, and to get it they eat tiny insects and spiders. They lap up insects along with nectar or catch them in flight. They also pluck insects from leaves and spiders right from their webs, hovering in the air all the while.

Most kinds of hummingbirds raise several broods of young a year. The birds pair up briefly to mate, and the males leave the nest-building and child-raising chores to the females. For many hummingbird species, the nest is a tiny cup, no bigger than a walnut shell. Most are made of moss and plant fibers, bound together with strands of silk stolen from spider webs. The female lays two tiny eggs, and she raises her chicks on an insect diet. Hummingbirds will defend their nests with amazing courage, even driving off hawks many times their size.

Adult hummingbirds travel alone, rather than in flocks. And many are common visitors to gardens. When a bird finds a good feeding spot, with plenty of flowers, it will stake out a territory and guard it jealously, driving other hummingbirds away.

Hummingbirds can often be seen near water, enjoying frequent baths. Sometimes they almost seem to be playing as they splash about. Many are also uncommonly curious. They will fly up to explore anything, even a person's clothing, if it is brightly colored. The fact that they can speed away so quickly if danger threatens may account for their boldness. Hummingbirds do fall victim to predators, however. Other birds, frogs, and even predatory insects such as the praying mantis might eat them, perhaps mistaking the little birds for large insects.

The boldness and curiosity of hummingbirds only adds to their charm. When Spanish explorers arrived in the Caribbean, hummingbirds were among the wonders they

reported. "The colors shine like those of the little birds artists paint to illuminate the margins of holy books," wrote one Spaniard. "They are hardy yet so little I would not dare tell of it if others had not seen them also."

Later, Europeans took a fancy to preserved hummingbirds, as ornaments on hats and other clothing. Thousands of the birds were killed. But today, people simply take delight in the beauty and charm of these fascinating and unique little birds. When a hummingbird visits the garden, it's always a welcome event.

THE PET PROJECT

"Come on, little buddies," Baloo called to Kit and Molly. "It's time to zoo-bee-doo to the zoo." Kit and Molly came running. Molly was wearing her new jacket with the chrome buttons.

But before they could leave, Molly's mother, Rebecca, stopped Baloo. "A rush delivery just came in," she told him. "It has to go out today."

"Aw, Becky, can't it wait?" Baloo looked at Kit's and Molly's downcast faces.

"I'm sorry," Rebecca said, stroking Molly's head. "It's a load of ice blocks for Nostralia. They're having a heat wave, and they need the ice right away."

Baloo saw Molly's chin quiver. "How about letting Molly fly to Nostralia with Kit and me? It's not very far, and we'll have a *cool* time, get it?" Baloo winked at Molly.

Soon Molly, Baloo, and Kit were all in Baloo's plane, the *Sea Duck*, heading for Nostralia's steamy jungle.

"Wow! Just look at all those trees," said Kit, gazing down at the tiny Nostralian airfield. Vines twisted among the tree branches,

and colorful flowers blazed against the green leaves.

"That's one big woodpile, little buddies," Baloo agreed as the *Sea Duck* touched down. "And it's full of strange animals."

While Baloo and Kit helped the eager Nostralians unload the ice, Molly wandered to the edge of the forest to sit in the shade.

She took off her jacket and placed it in her lap. Then she leaned against a tree and closed her eyes.

Something tugged at her jacket. Molly sat up, her heart pounding. Was it a strange animal? The something tugged again, and her jacket disappeared from her lap. Molly turned around carefully.

There was the strangest bird she had ever seen! It had a scrawny neck, long legs, and knobby knees. Its wings were small and stubby, and its big, round body was covered with feathers that shone like metal. And it was eating her jacket buttons!

"Stop that!" Molly grabbed her jacket, but the bird neatly nipped another button off! It looked so funny, Molly had to laugh.

"You're cute," she said. "Want to be my pet?"

Dangling her jacket, Molly led the bird to the *Sea Duck*. Baloo and Kit had finished unloading, and the cargo hold was empty.

Quickly Molly led the bird inside. "I think you should hide until we're home," she said, and she closed the door and slipped into the cockpit with Baloo and Kit.

Soon the *Sea Duck* was rising skyward, and the green land of Nostralia fell away far below.

"Now, that's the kind of job I like," Baloo leaned back in his seat. "Easy and breezy!"

A loud clank from the cargo hold interrupted him. Molly winced as Kit jumped up and threw open the cargo door.

"There's a bird in here—and it's eating the bolts on the door!" Kit cried. "It's a nostrich. I've read about them. They can't fly, and they'll eat anything. Especially anything metal," he added as the nostrich happily gulped down another bolt.

"How did it get in there?" Baloo looked suspiciously at Molly.

"It just followed me, Baloo." Molly squirmed. "It ate the buttons on my jacket. I thought it wanted to be my pet."

The nostrich waddled into the cockpit, smacking its beak as it swallowed two knobs and three dials from the control panel.

"Hey, cut it out, you metal-muncher!" Baloo yelped. "No one eats my plane! We're taking this can-cruncher back!"

"But, Baloo, it likes me!" Molly threw her arms around the nostrich's neck. Gurgling happily, it nipped a barrette from her hair and swallowed it.

Baloo just shook his head and banked the *Sea Duck*. Suddenly a hailstorm of bullets rattled against the plane's wings.

"It's Don Karnage!" Kit yelled. "And he's right on our tail flaps!"

"Hang on tight!" Baloo pulled back on the wheel, and the *Sea Duck* climbed straight as an arrow.

But soon Don Karnage was swooping

"Baloo, how could you?" Molly began to cry. "Just think of that poor helpless little nostrich with that mean old Don Karnage!"

"It's true, Baloo," Kit agreed. "We really should try to save it."

"Okay, okay," Baloo sighed. "But I wouldn't worry about that bolt-eating buzzard. I don't think it's very helpless."

Revving up his engines, Baloo zoomed after Don Karnage's plane. Molly and Kit stared out the window, worrying and watching, but Baloo hummed cheerfully.

"Just a few more minutes is all it should take," he said to himself.

Suddenly Don Karnage's plane began to dip and swerve. It tilted, jolted, jerked, dipped, bumped, and spun.

"Is that crazy pirate trying to dodge us?" Kit asked.

"I think he's trying to dodge the nostrich," Baloo laughed.

They watched Don Karnage flail his arms and yell at the nostrich, which was clamber-

alongside. Peering into the *Sea Duck*, he saw the nostrich's gleaming feathers. His eyes widened with greed.

"I, Don Karnage, dreaded pirate, demand that you hand over that valuable bird!" he cried, shaking his sword at Baloo. "Come and get it," Baloo yelled back.

Balancing on the seat of his plane, the pirate twirled a long rope with a pronged hook at one end. With a flourish, he flung it at the *Sea Duck* and anchored the hook in its wing. The plane tilted as the pirate climbed on board.

"Give me that bird!" Don Karnage cried, brandishing his sword.

To the pirate's surprise, Baloo didn't argue.

"Take it, Karny old pal," he said, hiding a smile.

With the nostrich under his arm, Don Karnage slid down the rope to his plane and unfastened the hook. As he sped away, he cheered in triumph.

ing over the plane, biting off large chunks. As the *Sea Duck* crew watched, pieces of the plane began to shake, rattle, and come apart. A wheel fell, then a door panel, then a hunk of the steering gear came off.

"Hey, Karnage, need some help?" Baloo called.

"Take back this preposterous pigeon!" Don Karnage shook his fist at Baloo and flung the nostrich overboard.

"Baloo, it can't fly! We have to save it!" Molly shrieked.

"Grab your airfoil and prepare for mission birdwatch!" Baloo commanded Kit. Kit opened his airfoil, jumped from the *Sea Duck*, and skimmed through the clouds. He swooped down and caught the nostrich. Holding it carefully under his arm, Kit trailed home behind the *Sea Duck* and floated to a gentle landing right behind it.

Baloo jumped from the plane. "I'm making one more delivery today—but I'm doing it on foot," he declared, leading the bird away.

Early the next day, Baloo woke Molly and Kit. He handed Molly her jacket with shiny new buttons sewn on. "It's zoo-bee-doo-bee-doo day," he said, "and I've got a surprise for you!"

Baloo led Kit and Molly past the elephants and giraffes, past the alligators and flamingos, to a big wide field. There, behind an unchewable safety-glass fence, stood the nostrich.

"Now coming to the zoo will be like visiting a friend," Molly laughed.

Baloo grinned. "I just hope he never invites us to stay for dinner," he said, looking at the nostrich happily munching away at a big pile of shiny buttons and bolts.

OUR FRAGILE EARTH—
It's the Only Home We Have

On April 22, 1990, some 200 million people in 140 countries joined in a common cause: to save the Earth. It was Earth Day 1990—an event that was a call for action to protect the fragile environment we live in.

There were street festivals, concerts, fairs, marches, and rallies. In France, people linked hands in a human chain that stretched 500 miles (805 kilometers). In Italy, 5,000 people lay down on a roadway to protest car exhaust. In Nepal, people climbed Mount Everest, picking up trash as they went. In Halifax, Nova Scotia, people gathered at sunrise and again at sunset to hear the singing of children's choirs and the chanting of a Micmac Indian medicine man.

In towns and cities across the United States, there were recycling demonstrations, tree planting ceremonies, and workshops on wildlife. In New York City, Washington, D.C., San Francisco, Boston, Chicago, and several other places, huge crowds gathered to hear concerts and speakers. At a Los Angeles high school, people sewed an Earth Day quilt. On the Maryland shore, they planted marsh grasses and set out nesting boxes for ducks.

At many of the events, the atmosphere was one of celebration—people were enjoying themselves on a beautiful spring day. But underlying the celebration was serious concern about the environment.

Concern about the environment isn't new. Twenty years earlier, on April 22, 1970, some 20 million Americans had called attention to threats to the environment in the first Earth Day. A few thousand people demonstrated in Washington, D.C. Elsewhere, people took part in local clean-ups and other activities that showed their concern.

While Earth Day 1970 had been much smaller than Earth Day 1990, it had helped make politicians aware that people were fed up with damage to the environment. New laws were passed to limit pollution, and the federal government set up the Environmental Protection Agency. But the effort petered out within a few years. The laws weren't enforced, and environmental damage continued to mount.

The 1980's saw a series of environmental disasters—including a nuclear power-plant accident in the Soviet Union that spewed radiation over much of Europe, and an oil spill off the coast of Alaska that was the worst oil spill ever in North American waters. At the same time, scientists began to warn of less visible but even more dangerous developments, including worldwide changes in the Earth's atmosphere and climate.

These events helped make people much more aware of the environment. They have begun to realize that life depends on a delicate balance of systems, and that the balance is in danger of being upset. They also realize that the environment is a global concern— no country and no person can ignore it.

That realization prompted Earth Day 1990, which was organized by a number of environmental groups. And it has also prompted new worldwide efforts to protect the fragile Earth. But solving the world's environmental problems won't be an easy task.

THREATENED WILDLIFE

There are more than 5 billion people in the world, and the number is growing so fast that the world's population is expected to double in less than 40 years. And as the population grows, people are taking over more and more wild areas and leaving less and less space for wildlife.

Tropical rain forests are home to the richest variety of plants and animals in the world —so rich that scientists haven't identified all the species that the forests hold. But these forests are being cut for timber and cleared to make room for farming at the rate of 40 to

Tropical rain forests are home to the richest variety of plants and animals in the world. But these forests are being destroyed to make room for agriculture at the rate of 40 to 50 million acres a year.

50 million acres a year. Forests in cooler climates are also being destroyed, by logging and development. Estimates released in 1990 show that the world has already lost 20 percent of its forests.

Forests aren't the only areas that are threatened. Great areas of grassland, such as the prairies of North America, have been plowed to grow crops or fenced as pasture for livestock. When grasslands are overgrazed or overcultivated, the soil washes or is blown away. The grasslands turn into wasteland, worthless as farmland or as a home for wild animals.

Wetlands—swamps, marshes, and bogs—are also threatened. These areas are home to many kinds of plants and animals, and coastal wetlands serve as nurseries for fish and other ocean creatures. But wetlands are being filled in for development. And in the ocean, the coral reefs that provide a rich habitat for thousands of animals are being buried in silt that runs off land that people have developed. The reefs are also mined for their coral and even dynamited by fishermen, to bring fish to the surface.

If these and other sensitive areas continue to be destroyed, the plants and animals that live in them will disappear. And even as people are destroying wildlife habitats, they are killing off animals directly.

Laws protect many endangered animals, but poachers continue to hunt them. Elephants are killed for their ivory. Pandas are killed for their skins. More killing results from carelessness. For example, commercial fishing nets scoop up rare turtles and marine mammals along with fish. Because these creatures need air, they drown when they are trapped in the nets.

Hundreds of plant and animal species have already disappeared, and every day more are in danger. In the United States alone, the number of species considered endangered or threatened rose from under 100 to more than 500 between 1970 and 1990. This is a great loss. Wild plants and animals are an important resource—they provide people with food, medicine, and other necessary substances. And the world will be a poorer place without the rich variety of life it now holds.

POLLUTION

In 1989 an oil spill off Alaska fouled hundreds of miles of shoreline and killed thousands of birds, fish, and other animals. It was a dramatic example of the damage pollution can do to wildlife. But pollution is damaging the environment every day, all over the world. And pollution harms people as well as wildlife.

Wetlands, streams, lakes, and ocean areas

Oil spills leave once-beautiful shorelines covered with globs of slime.

The Everglades, a wetland paradise in Florida, are being polluted by chemicals. This makes it difficult for its wildlife (such as this spoonbill) to survive.

are being contaminated by chemicals—toxic wastes produced by industry, and fertilizers and insecticides used in agriculture. The effects of this pollution can even be seen in the Everglades, a 10,000-square-mile (16,093-square-kilometer) swamp in Florida that is considered a U.S. national treasure.

In 1989, fish from the Everglades were declared unsafe to eat because of mercury contamination. And runoff from nearby farmlands, rich in fertilizers, has caused cattails and algae plants to multiply so fast that they have clogged waterways, making it impossible for fish, birds, and other animals to live. The environmental damage has also threatened the water supply of millions of people in south Florida, who obtain their water from the same system that feeds the swamp.

Air pollution is also having devastating effects. When people burn fossil fuels—coal, oil, and gasoline—the smoke and exhaust from the burning puts harmful chemicals such as ozone, sulfur dioxide, and nitrogen oxides in the air. These chemicals can build up in the air and can cause serious health problems. Cars that burn fuel more efficiently and produce cleaner exhaust have

been developed. But the air quality in many cities continues to worsen as their population grows.

Air pollution is also having harmful effects on the natural world. Some of the chemicals, in the form of sulfuric acid and nitric acid, are carried back to the ground in rain, fog, and snow. Precipitation that carries these pollutants is called *acid rain*. Acid rain is killing forests in North America and Europe. In the northeastern United States, it has made some lakes and streams so acid that life cannot survive in them.

Acid rain's effects on forests are complicated. Some trees are harmed directly. Acid rain damages the needles of the red spruce, for example, so that the trees can't turn sunlight into energy. In other cases, the effects are more subtle. The acid rain changes the chemistry of the soil, removing some elements that the trees need and producing others, such as aluminum, that can be toxic. Even if the trees don't die, they are weakened and are more likely to succumb to disease.

THE OZONE LAYER

Ozone in the air close to the ground is a dangerous pollutant; it's produced by car ex-

haust. But high in the atmosphere is a layer of ozone that performs an important job: It screens out much of the sun's harmful ultraviolet radiation. Without protection from the radiation, life on Earth couldn't survive. And the ozone layer is being destroyed by chemicals that people put in the air.

The ozone layer is thought to have formed billions of years ago, through the interaction of sunlight and oxygen. (The ozone produced by car exhaust doesn't rise to the upper atmosphere.) Because this interaction is still going on, the layer is constantly renewed. But since the 1970's, scientists have observed a thinning in the layer. The thinning is most serious over the Earth's poles—over Antarctica, the ozone level has dropped so much that scientists talk about a "hole" in the layer. But it's occurring worldwide.

Several pollutants are thought to be destroying the ozone. The most important are chlorofluorocarbons, or CFC's. CFC's are used as solvents, refrigerants, foaming agents in styrofoam and similar products, and propellants in aerosol sprays. When they are released into the air, they rise into the upper atmosphere and destroy the ozone.

The change in the ozone layer can't be seen or felt, but it could have serious results. Even a small increase in ultraviolet radiation can lead to higher rates of skin cancer and other health problems. The radiation can harm crops. And it can kill the tiny plants and animals that are at the bottom of the food chain. That might make survival impossible for larger animals.

Under an international treaty, 93 nations agreed in 1990 to phase out the use of CFC's, using other chemicals in their place. But some scientists fear that the chemicals used in place of CFC's will contribute to another problem: global warming.

GLOBAL WARMING

Air pollution and the thinning ozone are just the beginning of the problems that people have created in the atmosphere. Scientists have observed a worldwide warming trend that, they say, could be the beginning of a major change in the Earth's climate.

The problem is the *greenhouse effect*, caused by a buildup of carbon dioxide and other gases in the atmosphere. The gases are produced when fossil fuels are burned. And they act like the glass of a greenhouse to trap

The air in many large cities is polluted by the fumes from burning fossil fuels (coal, oil, and gas). These harmful chemicals can cause serious health problems in people.

heat—they let sunlight pass through to warm the Earth, but they don't permit heat to escape back into space.

The destruction of natural areas such as the tropical rain forests contributes to the greenhouse effect. When the forests are cleared for agriculture, people often burn the cut timber, releasing huge amounts of carbon dioxide into the air. And because trees and other plants absorb carbon dioxide, cutting forests means that more carbon dioxide will remain in the atmosphere.

There is debate about how serious the greenhouse effect will be. Most scientists agree that even small changes in the world's average annual temperature could bring drought to fertile farmlands, dry up important inland waterways, and cause forests to die out. And some believe that the Earth will warm enough to melt the polar ice caps. That would raise sea levels, and coastal areas would be flooded.

The Earth has seen major climate changes in the past. But these changes took place over very long periods of time, and plants and animals were able to adjust to them. Now carbon dioxide and the other greenhouse gases are building up rapidly in the atmosphere as people burn more fossil fuels to run their cars and factories, heat their homes, and produce electricity. If the buildup continues, the Earth's climate may change too rapidly for life to adjust.

TRASH AND TOXIC WASTES

As the world's population has grown, disposing of household trash and the toxic wastes produced by industry has become a major problem. If trash and toxic wastes are burned, they pollute the air. If they are dumped at sea, they pollute the ocean. And if they are buried, pollution can seep through the ground, contaminating groundwater.

The huge amounts of trash that are discarded, especially in wealthy countries, are a symptom of another problem: the waste of the world's resources. The Earth has only so much ore to produce metal; only so much petroleum to produce fuel, fertilizer, and plastic; only so many trees to produce lumber and paper. People are rapidly using up these resources.

WHAT CAN BE DONE?

Alarm over the mounting damage to the environment has sparked new efforts to protect the fragile Earth. But scientists who have studied the problems warn that halting

Chemicals that pollute the air may be carried back to the ground in rain, fog, and snow. The pollutants formed when fossil fuels are burned create "acid rain"; this type of precipitation can kill trees. Other pollutants result from chemical pesticides and can cause twisted beaks in birds.

the damage to the environment will be a huge job, and that everyone must take part.

In many areas, there are new regulations to protect the environment. The United States passed a new clean air law in 1990. It requires car makers, power plants, and other polluters to meet tougher standards on pollution. California, where air pollution is a major problem, has passed rules that order strict auto-emissions controls and restrict the use of cars in crowded areas. Many towns and cities are starting to recycle some of their trash, so that paper, glass, metal, and plastic can be used again instead of just thrown away. And several countries have formed a group to study the greenhouse problem.

Individuals are also getting involved. As people become more aware of the dangers to the environment, they are trying to help. The steps are often simple—carpooling to work, recycling trash, turning off lights. These small steps make a difference when millions of people take them, saving thousands of acres of forest and preventing the release of millions of tons of pollutants into the air.

People are also speaking out about environmental issues, urging governments to protect wild areas and limit development. Membership in environmental and conservation groups is growing. And "green" political parties, which support conservation, have become important in many countries.

So far, however, these efforts have barely made a dent in the Earth's environmental problems. Many countries are reluctant to limit the use of fossil fuels—they are so important to modern life that doing so could hurt a country's economy. And CFC's and similar gases that have already been released into the atmosphere will continue to do harm for years to come.

Many people believe that the only way to lessen air pollution, damage to the ozone layer, and the greenhouse effect is to cut down on the use of fossil fuels and other activities that produce harmful gases. But the world's population continues to grow. Each year more people need food, energy, and living space.

Thus halting the damage to the environment will be a huge job. It may require some sacrifices by everyone. But many people believe that the job must be done if life on our fragile Earth is to survive. Their hope was that Earth Day 1990 would mark the start of a new chapter in the Earth's history, one in which people would become the caretakers, not the destroyers, of the natural world.

Disposing of household trash has become a major problem. And if plastic items are tossed in the ocean and wash up to shore, seals and other animals can get tangled up in the plastic and die.

WHAT YOU CAN DO

Young people all around the world are taking the lead in new efforts to protect the environment. Here are some of the things they're doing:

• In 1987, fifth graders in Closter, New Jersey, started a group called Kids Against Pollution to protest the use of polystyrene food containers. This foamy plastic, widely used by fast-food restaurants, doesn't break down and produces harmful fumes when it burns. Since then, the campaign has taken off—800 chapters of the group have formed across the United States and Europe.

• Several programs give schoolchildren a way to save the tropical rain forests. A Swedish program called the International Children's Rain Forest Program and another run by the Nature Conservancy, a U.S. group, use kids' donations to buy rain forest land. Kids often raise the money by collecting and selling recyclable trash.

• Children from all around the world designed posters in support of the environment in 1990. The posters were shown on a television special, "Earth '90," that was broadcast in June. Children's sing-ing groups appeared along with rock and pop stars on the show.

• Third-grade students in Wisconsin cleaned up a trash-filled pond, planted trees and flowers around it, and created a wildlife refuge. Students in New Mexico, Utah, California, and other areas have done similar projects.

• Kids in many communities have led recycling and clean-up drives, picking up trash from beaches, parks, and roadsides.

What can *you* do to help save the environment? Plant a tree. Save water—just turning off the faucet while you brush your teeth can save as much as 10 gallons of water. Save energy—turn off lights and walk, bike, or use public transportation instead of the family car. Recycle newspapers and glass and metal containers instead of throwing them away. Use products that can be used again—don't buy throwaway dishes and utensils, and take your own shopping bag to the grocery store. And get involved with groups in your area that are working to save the environment.

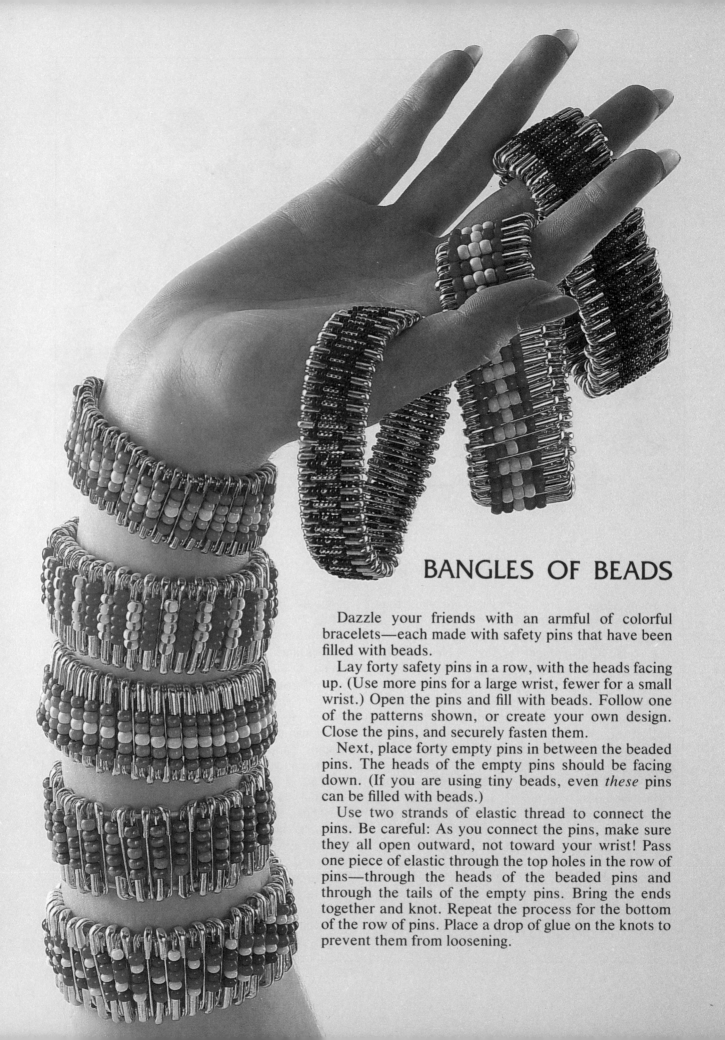

BANGLES OF BEADS

Dazzle your friends with an armful of colorful bracelets—each made with safety pins that have been filled with beads.

Lay forty safety pins in a row, with the heads facing up. (Use more pins for a large wrist, fewer for a small wrist.) Open the pins and fill with beads. Follow one of the patterns shown, or create your own design. Close the pins, and securely fasten them.

Next, place forty empty pins in between the beaded pins. The heads of the empty pins should be facing down. (If you are using tiny beads, even *these* pins can be filled with beads.)

Use two strands of elastic thread to connect the pins. Be careful: As you connect the pins, make sure they all open outward, not toward your wrist! Pass one piece of elastic through the top holes in the row of pins—through the heads of the beaded pins and through the tails of the empty pins. Bring the ends together and knot. Repeat the process for the bottom of the row of pins. Place a drop of glue on the knots to prevent them from loosening.

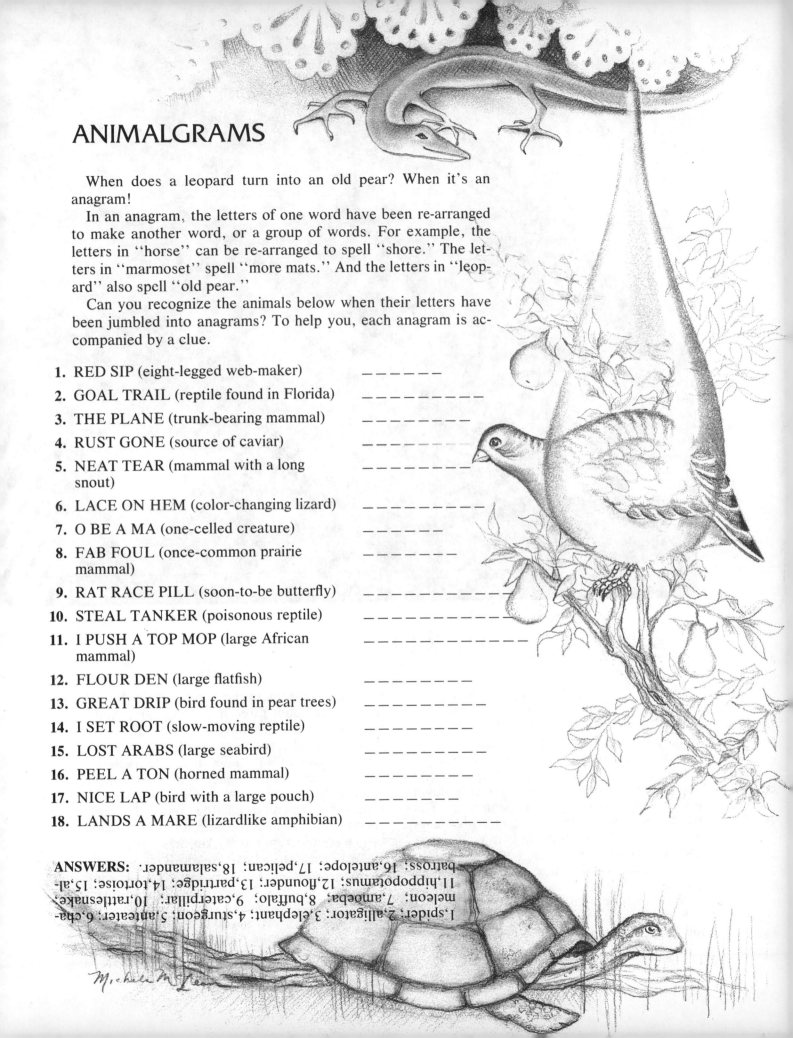

ANIMALGRAMS

When does a leopard turn into an old pear? When it's an anagram!

In an anagram, the letters of one word have been re-arranged to make another word, or a group of words. For example, the letters in "horse" can be re-arranged to spell "shore." The letters in "marmoset" spell "more mats." And the letters in "leopard" also spell "old pear."

Can you recognize the animals below when their letters have been jumbled into anagrams? To help you, each anagram is accompanied by a clue.

1. RED SIP (eight-legged web-maker) _ _ _ _ _ _
2. GOAL TRAIL (reptile found in Florida) _ _ _ _ _ _ _ _ _
3. THE PLANE (trunk-bearing mammal) _ _ _ _ _ _ _ _
4. RUST GONE (source of caviar) _ _ _ _ _ _ _ _
5. NEAT TEAR (mammal with a long snout) _ _ _ _ _ _ _ _
6. LACE ON HEM (color-changing lizard) _ _ _ _ _ _ _ _ _
7. O BE A MA (one-celled creature) _ _ _ _ _ _
8. FAB FOUL (once-common prairie mammal) _ _ _ _ _ _ _
9. RAT RACE PILL (soon-to-be butterfly) _ _ _ _ _ _ _ _ _ _ _
10. STEAL TANKER (poisonous reptile) _ _ _ _ _ _ _ _ _ _
11. I PUSH A TOP MOP (large African mammal) _ _ _ _ _ _ _ _ _ _ _ _
12. FLOUR DEN (large flatfish) _ _ _ _ _ _ _ _
13. GREAT DRIP (bird found in pear trees) _ _ _ _ _ _ _ _ _
14. I SET ROOT (slow-moving reptile) _ _ _ _ _ _ _ _
15. LOST ARABS (large seabird) _ _ _ _ _ _ _ _ _
16. PEEL A TON (horned mammal) _ _ _ _ _ _ _ _
17. NICE LAP (bird with a large pouch) _ _ _ _ _ _ _
18. LANDS A MARE (lizardlike amphibian) _ _ _ _ _ _ _ _ _ _

ANSWERS: 1,spider; 2,alligator; 3,elephant; 4,sturgeon; 5,anteater; 6,chameleon; 7,amoeba; 8,buffalo; 9,caterpillar; 10,rattlesnake; 11,hippopotamus; 12,flounder; 13,partridge; 14,tortoise; 15,albatross; 16,antelope; 17,pelican; 18,salamander.

THE THRILL OF THE RIDE

Slowly, the car lurches higher and higher. It's above the treetops now, supported only by a spindly wooden frame. Your heart is beating faster, and your palms begin to sweat —something dreadful is about to happen.

Suddenly, the car swings around a bend and takes you over the top, plunging down toward the ground at 60 miles an hour. The wind whips your hair back and brings tears to your eyes. Your stomach is in your throat and your heart is in your knees. Your mouth is wide open, and you're screaming for all you're worth.

And you love every minute of it!

For sheer thrills and terrifying chills, nothing beats a roller coaster. Variations of this exciting amusement-park ride have been around for about three hundred years. And while roller coasters have had their ups and downs over the years, today they are more popular than at any time since the 1920's. New coasters—ever higher and faster, with steeper drops and more devilish twists and turns—are opening all the time. People spend hours in line, waiting for a ride that lasts a couple of minutes. And when the ride is over, they rush back to the line to wait again.

SLIPPERY BEGINNINGS

It was the Russians who came up with the basic idea behind the roller coaster. The first

coal from mines at the top of Mt. Pisgah to Mauch Chunk, at the foot of the mountain. As a passenger ride, it carried people to the top of the mountain and then sent them down again. Traveling at just 5 miles (8 kilometers) an hour, the Mauch Chunk Railway was tame by the standards of today's coasters. But the scenery was beautiful, and the ride was an instant success.

Soon artificial coasting courses were being built. In these rides, the slides were made up of fat rollers placed one after another, conveyor-belt style. The coasting-course fad didn't last long—but the name "roller coaster" survived.

Like the earlier Russian Mountains, these roller coasters carried people straight down —there were no stomach-flipping ups and downs. The first ride that resembled a modern coaster, with artificial hills and valleys, appeared in 1884. It was the Switchback Gravity Pleasure Railway, built by La-Marcus A. Thompson at Coney Island in Brooklyn, New York. In it, riders boarded a ten-person wheeled car and were carried down an undulating (up-and-down) track at six miles (10 kilometers) an hour.

People lined up to take a five-cent ride on

coasters were actually ice slides built in St. Petersburg (now Leningrad) in the 1600's. The slides, supported by wooden frames and angled at about 50 degrees, provided a slick, fast surface for sleds. Riders climbed to a platform at the top and then shot straight down the slide at thrilling speeds.

The French adopted the concept but redesigned the rides. They added tiny wheels to the sleds, so that ice wasn't needed and the slides could be enjoyed year-round. The first of the French slides, which were called Russian Mountains, was introduced in Paris in the early 1800's.

A half century later, the popular rides spread to the United States. The first U.S. coaster, which began operating in 1870, was actually a converted railway in Pennsylvania. It originally had been designed to carry

THE SCIENCE OF THRILLS

A day at an amusement park doesn't seem like an educational activity. But at many parks, it's not uncommon to see science students scurrying from ride to ride with notebooks. That's because the rides—and especially the big roller coasters—demonstrate some basic principles of physics.

Once the cars in a roller coaster reach the top of the first hill, for example, gravity (which pulls downward) is the only force that sends them speeding along the tracks. That means that the speed of a coaster ride is closely related to the height of the first hill—the bigger the drop, the more speed the cars pick up as they plunge down. This is why taller coasters (and the tallest is as high as a 20-story building) provide more thrills.

Speed also makes it possible for the cars to flip upside-down through corkscrews and loops. As long as the cars are traveling fast enough, centrifugal force (which pushes outward) will keep you glued to your seat, even when the car is at the top of the loop.

The big loops on coasters aren't perfect circles. They are teardrop shapes called *clothoid loops*. In a perfect circle, the cars would slow down too much at the top of the loop. Then the force of gravity might be stronger than the centrifugal force, causing passengers to fall out of their seats. The elongated shape of the clothoid loop keeps the cars moving faster at the top, increasing centrifugal force.

Centrifugal force also acts on the cars when they whip around curves. That's why roller coaster tracks are banked, or angled, on curves—if the tracks were level, centrifugal force might send the cars flying off.

Designers calculate these forces carefully when they build a new coaster. They know just how fast the cars will be traveling at each point and how much each turn must be banked. That, combined with rider harnesses and rigorous operating and inspection standards, makes roller coasters far safer than they look.

the new invention, and Thompson soon was taking in about $700 a day. It was clear that lots of people were willing to pay money to be scared. Soon other amusement park owners were clamoring for similar rides, and a roller-coaster boom began.

By 1920, most amusement parks had some kind of roller coaster. The designers of these coasters made many improvements on Thompson's first design. For example, the Switchback Railway track followed a straight course (rather than the circular course used by today's coasters), and the cars had no power. That meant that the cars had to be pushed to the top of the track after each ride. Circular tracks and power lifts were among the first refinements made in roller-coaster design.

Then designers concentrated on making each new coaster bigger, steeper, faster—in other words, more terrifying—than the one before. The scarier a coaster was, it seemed, the more people it drew. An especially terrifying roller coaster was the Coney Island Cyclone, perhaps the most well-known coaster of all time. World-famous aviator Charles Lindbergh declared it to be "a greater thrill than flying an airplane at top speed."

Another heart-stopper was built at Playland, in Rye, New York. It was 90 feet (27 meters) high, and at one point the cars plunged underground—adding an extra thrill to the ride and making this the first coaster to go underground.

But in the 1930's, the roller-coaster boom came to an end. An economic depression settled in, and many people were out of work. Fewer people went to amusement

On King Cobra (Kings Island, Ohio), riders wear cushioned harnesses and remain standing up during the entire looping ride.

Magnum XL-200 (Cedar Point Park, Sandusky, Ohio) is billed as the tallest, non-looping steel coaster, with a 20-story plunge.

parks—they just didn't have the money for rides. As park attendance dropped, roller coasters stood idle. Many were torn down.

After the Depression and World War II, however, the situation began to change. A new kind of amusement park—the theme park—appeared. Disneyland, which opened in Anaheim, California, in 1955, was the first of these parks. Disneyland introduced its first roller coaster, the Matterhorn Bobsleds, in 1958, and the ride was instantly popular.

Soon other theme parks were being built. And more often than not, roller coasters were the centerpieces of these parks. Just as in the 1920's, people wanted the thrills and excitement that only a roller coaster could provide.

TERRIFYING TWISTS

Like amusement parks of the past, parks of today are constantly competing to have the biggest, tallest, fastest, and scariest roller coaster. And today's roller coasters provide thrills that riders of the 1890's could never have imagined. For one thing, they travel at up to ten times the speed of the early coasters.

Today's roller coasters don't just send riders around curves and up and down a few hills, either. The cars hurtle through corkscrews and spirals, turn upside-down in complete loops, and plunge riders into total darkness. And some coasters are even designed to carry riders standing up.

Many of these hair-raising designs were

made possible by the development of tubular steel tracks in the late 1950's. These tracks make coaster rides faster, smoother, and quieter. Because the wheels of the cars grip the tubular tracks from top to bottom, rather than riding on top as they do on flat rails, the new tracks also allow designers to throw in a whole series of inverted loops and corkscrews. And they make possible some other terrifying twists. In the Iron Dragon, at Cedar Point in Sandusky, Ohio, the cars are suspended from an overhead steel track. They swing out around turns and skim over water and treetops—with nothing between riders and the ground.

But for some roller-coaster enthusiasts, there's nothing like an old-fashioned wooden coaster, or "woodie." Loops and corkscrews are fine, but the jolts, shakes, and roar of a woodie add extra thrills to the ride. Thus woodies are still being built. Many are new designs. The Texas Giant, at Six Flags Over Texas in Arlington, is typical of these. It takes riders 40 stories into the air on the first hill—and there are 20 more plunges still to come.

There's also great interest in restoring old coasters and in re-creating some of the best old designs. The Coney Island Cyclone, famous in the late 1920's, is still running and has been named a national landmark. The Raging Wolf Bobs, in Aurora, Ohio, is a replica of a famous coaster built in Chicago's Riverview Park in the 1920's. There are even plans for a "park of the past"—Electric Park, near Indianapolis, Indiana. Set to open in 1991, it will feature several designs from famous amusement parks of the 1920's.

Old or new, it seems that roller coasters have a special appeal. What heart-stopping twist will coaster designers think up next? Whatever it is, one thing is certain: People will line up for a chance to experience the thrill of the ride.

The Texas Giant (Six Flags Over Texas, Arlington) opened in 1990. A "woodie," it's high, fast, and wild.

SPIDER WEBS: STRONG AS STEEL

Covered with dew, a spider's web hangs from a branch like a jeweled necklace. The silk that forms the web is feather-light and looks fragile and delicate in the early morning rays of the sun. Yet this amazing material is actually stronger than steel and, at the same time, as elastic as a rubber band.

People have never been able to make a material with all the wonderful properties of natural spider silk. But now, using new techniques, researchers are trying to produce the silk commercially. If they succeed, spider silk may one day be used in everything from bullet-proof vests to stockings.

SILKEN NETS

Spiders are hunters that catch and eat insects. (Spiders themselves aren't insects.

They belong to a group called the arachnids, which also includes scorpions and ticks.) All spiders have special glands that produce spider silk, which is a protein. The silk is spun by being forced out as a liquid through tiny fingerlike organs called spinnerets. The liquid hardens into fine, tough threads after hitting the air.

Most spiders use their silk to build webs that will capture their prey. And there are almost as many different kinds of webs as there are different kinds of spiders. Some webs consist of just a strand or two of silk; others are a jumbled tangle of threads. Some spiders spin broad sheets that hang horizontally in bushes and trees. Still others construct tunnel-like traps of silk.

The master builders of the spider world

are the orb-weavers. "Orb" means "circle," and these spiders weave circular, wheel-like webs. Strong, dry threads, which act as spokes, run out from the center of the web and anchor it in place. The fine, sticky threads that spiral around the circle are coated with a sort of watery glue, to trap the spider's prey.

But web-building isn't the only use that spiders have for their silk—in fact, a few spiders don't build webs at all. Spiders can spin several different kinds of silk, each having a different purpose. All are made of the same basic protein, but they have different qualities.

After a spider catches an insect, for example, it wraps its prey in a special binding silk and stores it to eat later. Female spiders wrap their eggs in a soft, protective case made of another type of silk. When the baby spiders hatch, they spin long streamers of silk that catch the wind. The babies are lifted into the air and carried off, sometimes for many miles. Wherever they land, they make their homes.

All spiders also make a fine but extremely strong silk that they trail as a dragline—a sort of safety line. If you've ever startled a spider, you may have seen it drop to the ground and then, a moment later, scuttle back up its dragline to its web. Most of the cobwebs that people find in their homes are draglines that spiders have left behind.

SPIDER-SILK STOCKINGS

The remarkable properties of spider silk have long fascinated people. The silk is amazingly strong and flexible. When a spider web stops a flying insect, it's the equivalent of stopping an airliner with a rope net. The silk doesn't break because it's stronger than the best steel wire and can stretch to nearly twice its length before it snaps. And it's practically rot-proof.

Spider silk is so amazing that people would like to produce it commercially, in the same way that the silk of another creature—the silk moth—is used. Fibers produced by the silk moth caterpillar (or silkworm) are the basis of silk fabric. But raising spiders for their silk is a very different matter from raising silk moth caterpillars.

Unlike the caterpillars, which eat leaves, the spiders must have live insect food. Also, spiders attack each other as well as insects. And it would take many, many spiders to produce a useful amount of silk. By one estimate, 5,000 large spiders would have to spin day and night to make the silk for one dress. Thus in the past, spider silk has been used in only a few ways—to make cross hairs in gunsights, for example.

Now, however, some scientists think there may be a way to produce spider silk commercially. The technique involves genetic engineering (altering the material within cells that carries inherited traits). With genetic engineering, bacteria might be programmed to produce spider-silk protein.

The bacteria would be grown in big vats, and the protein would be extracted and spun into thread through mechanical spinnerets. If the plan works, spider-silk stockings may be the fashion craze of the future.

October 3, 1990: Germany is one nation again and jubilant crowds gather at the Brandenburg Gate—long a symbol of the division of East and West Berlin.

GERMANY: A COUNTRY REUNITED

At 12:01 A.M. on October 3, 1990, after 45 years of separation, East Germany and West Germany were reunited. It was the climax of a series of dramatic events that brought the two Germanys, divided at the end of World War II, together at last.

Just a year earlier, few people would have imagined that the reunification of Germany was likely. But in 1989, change began to shake the Communist countries of Eastern Europe—including East Germany. Repressive Communist governments buckled to pressure for reform and democracy. It was this sweeping movement that, eventually, made German reunification possible.

The new Germany seemed likely to be one of the most important countries in Europe— and the world. Yet, after years of life under opposing political and economic systems, Germans faced some difficult adjustments.

A DIVIDED GERMANY

Compared to other European countries, the German nation was formed late in his-

tory. In 1871, a group of separate German states was unified by force by Otto von Bismarck, chancellor to the Prussian ruler William I. Germany quickly became one of Europe's strongest powers. Germany's ambitions eventually led to World War I (1914–18), in which it was defeated by Britain, France, and the United States.

The harsh peace terms exacted from Germany at the end of World War I hurt the country's economy and made many Germans resentful. This contributed to the rise of the Nazi dictator Adolf Hitler in the 1930's. During World War II, Hitler's armies overran most of Europe. The Nazis were notorious not only for their aggression but for their brutality and the atrocities they committed. During the war years, they killed some six million Jews, along with thousands of Gypsies and other minorities.

In 1945, Hitler was defeated by the chief Allied Powers: Britain, France, the Soviet Union, and the United States. War-torn and devastated by heavy bombing, Germany was

80

divided into four occupation zones. The Soviets controlled the easternmost zone, and the other Allies controlled zones in the west.

Tensions soon developed between the Allies. As a Communist country, the Soviet Union had little in common with the Western allies. The Soviets were dedicated to the spread of Communism, while the three other powers hoped to see democracy flourish in Germany. This split marked the beginning of the Cold War, which would dominate world events for many years.

As a result of these tensions, there was no peace conference at the end of the war. Cooperation between the Allies ended completely in 1948, and the question of Germany's future remained unsettled. As they had elsewhere in Eastern Europe, the Soviets set up a Communist state in East Germany (the German Democratic Republic) in 1949. Meanwhile, the three western zones were combined to form West Germany (the Federal Republic of Germany).

Under a democratic government and with economic help from Western countries, West Germany began to recover from the devastating effects of the war. It developed a healthy, booming economy based on free markets and private enterprise. In the 1950's, it strengthened its ties to other Western countries by joining the North Atlantic Treaty Organization (NATO) and the European Economic Community (Common Market).

East Germany remained linked to the Soviet Union, joining the Warsaw Pact and Communist economic groups. Its government controlled the economy and most aspects of life. Recovery from the war was slow. And after Soviet forces crushed a revolt in East Germany in 1953, the system became even more tightly controlled.

Faced with a life of drabness and repression, many East Germans left for the West. By 1961 they were leaving at the rate of 1,000 a day, and East Germany had developed a serious labor shortage. The East German government abruptly decided to stop the flood by sealing its entire border with West Germany. Barbed wire was strung along the border, and machine-gun-carrying soldiers patrolled it. On each side, Germans were cut off from friends and family.

THE BEGINNING OF CHANGE

For the next 28 years, divided Germany remained a symbol of the tensions of the Cold War. But slowly, change began to come to the Communist world. It started in the Soviet Union, which took small steps toward greater democracy and economic freedom in the late 1980's. Soon it became clear that the Soviets would no longer enforce the Communist rule of Eastern Europe with armed force. In country after country of Eastern Europe, demonstrators demanded freedom. And in country after country, they won it.

East Germany's Communist rulers remained firmly opposed to change. But in mid-1989, thousands of East Germans began to escape to the West through Hungary, which had relaxed its border controls. And East Germans who stayed behind took to the streets in huge protests. In October, East German leader Erich Honecker was forced to resign, along with most of his government.

And then something else remarkable happened: On November 9, East Germany opened its border with West Germany. Soon it was clear that the Communist rule of East Germany had collapsed. And the reunification of Germany, which had seemed so distant only months before, suddenly seemed inevitable.

At first people thought that reunification would take many years to achieve. But several factors forced the pace to quicken. After years of failed Communist policies, the East German economy was near collapse. And East Germans were pouring into West Germany in huge numbers. West Germany was hard pressed to provide them with housing, jobs, and social services. Maybe faster reunification would end the flood of refugees and help the East German economy.

But reunification raised complicated questions. In East Germany, changing to a market economy would mean that many inefficient, state-run businesses would close, bringing widespread unemployment. Government workers, too—including members of East Germany's infamous secret police—would be out of work.

There were questions that involved other countries as well. Some of Germany's neighbors, especially Poland, feared that a united Germany might try to reclaim territory it had lost in the war. And while relations between the Soviet Union and the West were improving, there were still tensions. Soviet troops were stationed in East Germany, and NATO forces were stationed in West Germany. The United States and other Western powers

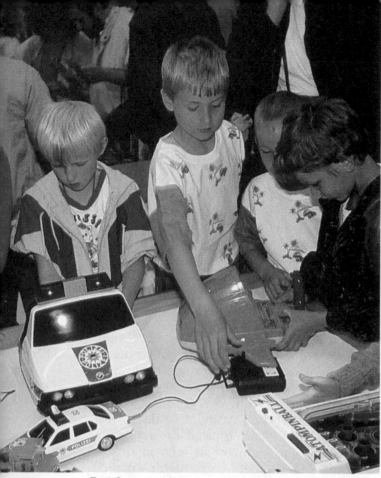

East German children eagerly examine West German toys. There were great differences in the quality of the goods produced in the two countries.

Then, on July 16, the Soviet Union dropped its objection to German membership in NATO. In an agreement negotiated by West German Chancellor Helmut Kohl and Soviet President Mikhail Gorbachev, the Soviets also agreed to withdraw their troops from Germany over a three- to four-year period. In exchange, Kohl agreed that Germany would help pay for the withdrawal, would limit its own troop strength, and wouldn't allow NATO troops or nuclear weapons in what had been East Germany.

The last hurdle to full unification had been cleared. On September 12, the World War II Allies and the two Germanys signed a peace treaty that would restore sovereignty to a future united Germany. And on October 3, West Germany and East Germany at last joined to form a single nation.

AFTER UNIFICATION

Helmut Kohl was named the first chancellor of the new Germany. And on December 2, 1990, Kohl won the first free all-German elections in 58 years. His government, and all Germans, faced a future that was bright but far from trouble-free.

West Germany had developed one of the strongest economies in the world. But East Germany's roads, railroads, and telephone system needed rebuilding. Banks had to be compensated for the currency exchange. Huge amounts would have to be paid in unemployment and other social benefits for East Germans who were thrown out of work by the switch to a market economy. These and other costs of unification, such as paying for Soviet troop withdrawals, were expected to be well over $200 billion—a staggering sum.

There were social problems, too. East Germans feared that they would be treated as second-class citizens. West Germans worried that East Germans, already working for low wages, would take their jobs. Some West Germans complained that East Germans were too used to being taken care of by the state and were unwilling to work hard. East Germans complained that West Germans were cold and cared only for material things.

Most people agreed that Germany would be able to put these problems behind it and that, when it did, it would be one of the most important countries in Europe. In fact, some

said that Germany should decide whether to remain in NATO (which meant that it probably would remain). The Soviets wanted a united Germany to be neutral.

In February, the two Germanys and representatives of the four World War II Allies met in Ottawa, Canada, and agreed on a framework for reunification. First, East and West Germany would agree on the domestic aspects. Then they would meet with the Allies to settle the international questions.

As this "two-plus-four" process got under way, events moved forward with dizzying speed. East Germany's first free elections were held in March, and a coalition led by the Christian Democratic Union swept the vote. Since the Christian Democrats were also in power in West Germany, this helped smooth the path to unification. Both Germanys soon agreed to honor the postwar border with Poland. And on July 1, they officially merged their economies. East Germans were able to exchange their nearly worthless currency for West German marks.

BERLIN—AGAIN THE CAPITAL

As the two Germanys united in 1990, no city had greater reason to celebrate than Berlin—because no city had suffered more during Germany's troubled years.

Before World War II, Berlin was Germany's capital and one of Europe's most famous cities, known for its beautiful boulevards and buildings and for its sophistication. But the city suffered terribly in the closing days of the war, when bombing reduced wide sections to rubble.

When the Allied Powers divided Germany into occupation zones after the war, Berlin (which was in the Soviet sector) was also divided into four zones, with the Soviets controlling East Berlin. Then, in June, 1948, the Soviets attempted to force the Western allies out of West Berlin. All land routes into the city were blocked by Soviet troops. For eleven months, the Western allies flew food and other supplies to the city in a massive airlift.

Eventually, the Soviets backed down. But Berlin's troubles were far from over. When East Germany closed its border with West Germany in 1961, the East Germans built a towering concrete wall that divided Berlin in two. People were allowed to cross only at tightly controlled checkpoints, and few were let through. The Berlin Wall became a stage for heroism and tragedy as determined East Germans tried to escape to freedom in the West. Many succeeded. But many others didn't, and some were killed in the attempt.

To most of the world, the Berlin Wall was a symbol of Communist repression. U.S. President John F. Kennedy expressed the feeling of the free world when he visited West Berlin soon after the wall was built and announced, "I am a Berliner." Even when tensions between East and West eased in the 1970's, the Wall stood as a grim reminder of the deep opposition between the two sides.

There matters stood until 1989, when Berlin, along with the rest of East Germany, became caught up in the changes that were sweeping through the Communist world. On the night of November 9, a rumor spread through the city: the East German government had opened its borders

Westerners went East and Easterners went West, and everyone found out what was behind the Berlin Wall.

with the West. East Berliners went to the Wall to see if the rumor was true—and found that it was.

Once again, Berliners could move freely through their city. Within days, thousands were pouring back and forth, and East German troops had begun to tear down the infamous 29-mile (47-kilometer) wall. The parts that remained became the scene of joyful celebrations. Gradually, subway lines and other links between the two parts of the city were reopened.

With reunification, Berlin once again became the capital of Germany. The city's Reichstag building became the seat of Parliament, as it had been before the country was divided. And as united Germany's black, red, and gold flag was raised at the Reichstag just after midnight on October 3, bells pealed and fireworks exploded in the night sky. Berliners all over the city celebrated the end of their long ordeal.

people feared that Germany would dominate Europe. They looked to the past—to the Germany of World Wars I and II.

But people who looked to the future saw that a united and democratic Germany, with close ties to other European countries, could be a valuable member of the world community. Thus, as Germans celebrated on October 3, people around the world wished them well.

THE DOUBTING DALMATIAN

It was a dark and stormy night. Rain pounded against the windows, and the wind whistled through the eaves. But inside a warm fire blazed, and fifteen Dalmatian puppies sat around the television watching the famous detective chase a ghostly hound across the English moors.

The smallest puppy forgot himself for an instant and raced to the screen, barking wildly.

"Oh, Lucky, do pipe down! We can't hear a thing," said Nanny kindly. She was perched on the edge of her chair, holding the sock she was knitting close to her face in case the scene got too scary to watch.

Suddenly there was a bright flash outside. Fifteen puppies yelped and dove under Nanny's big armchair. Nanny tried to sound confident. "Silly puppies! That was just a bit of

lightning." One nose poked out from under the chair, but suddenly a clap of thunder shook the house. The lights flickered and then went out.

"Now don't worry, little ones," said Nanny, getting up and feeling her way slowly across the dark room. "I'll just get some candles, and we'll be right as rain in no time."

Freckles shivered under the chair in the dark. "I just wish mom and dad hadn't gone on holiday with Roger and Anita," she said.

"Me, too," sighed her brother Rolly. "They won't be back until tomorrow."

Just then, a light flickered on the far side of the room as Nanny lit the candle. The light made them all feel braver, and one by one they crawled out from under the chair.

Another flash filled the night sky with a

ghostly light. Nanny raised her candle toward the front door and let out a terrified gasp. Silhouetted against the glass door panel was a strange, dark form. Lucky growled low in his throat, and the other puppies pushed up close to Nanny. Another boom of thunder shook the house just as the doorbell rang.

"Who is it? Who's there?" called Nanny, her voice edged with fear.

"It's Anita's Aunt Ida. From America," said a woman's voice. "Please let me in."

"Well, I can't leave her out in this storm," Nanny muttered to herself, opening the door. Lucky growled again as a tall, dripping form in a tweed coat, carrying two large suitcases, rushed past him into the hall. Aunt Ida —or whoever she was—set her dripping bags down, plopped herself on the stairs, and began pulling off an enormous pair of black rubber boots.

"Didn't Anita tell you I was coming?" she asked. "I wrote her well over a month ago.

And she wrote back saying she'd love to have me stay." The mysterious woman dug around in her purse and finally produced a letter.

Nanny studied it closely in the candlelight. "But this letter doesn't say when," she said suspiciously.

"Well, I sent a postcard about two weeks ago telling Anita that I would be staying in London with her tonight. I assumed that I missed her reply, since I've been touring around England."

"Well, this is a mystery," said Nanny. "I'm sure she didn't know you were coming. You see, she's gone trekking with Master Roger for the weekend. They were planning to camp outdoors tonight, so there's no way to phone, but she'll be home tomorrow. You can stay here tonight. Meanwhile, would you like a cup of tea?"

"That would be lovely," said the stranger, and she followed Nanny into the kitchen, trailed by a crowd of very curious puppies.

Suddenly the lights in the house came back on. "Thank goodness!" said Rolly. He joined Lucky and Patch, who had stayed behind in the hallway to sniff Aunt Ida's wet suitcases and big rubber boots.

"I don't think she's Anita's American aunt," said Lucky.

"Why not?" asked Patch. "Nanny believes her. And what about that letter from Anita?"

"Forged!" said Lucky.

"What about the American accent?" asked Rolly.

"Faked," countered Lucky.

"Then who is she?" asked Patch.

"Elementary, my dear brother," began Lucky. "Let's use deductive reasoning."

"Oh, I get it," said Rolly. "Like the famous detective on television. Okay. What's your first deduction?"

Lucky sniffed again at her boots. "First notice these boots. They aren't American. They're Wellington boots, made in England. And that coat is made of English tweed. I don't think Aunt Ida is from America at all!"

"So what!" said Rolly.

"Well, if she's not Anita's Aunt Ida from America, then who is she?" Lucky asked.

Lucky looked at Aunt Ida's biggest bag. "Look at this," he said. "Aunt Ida said she had been touring around England. There's a bus tag stuck to the side of this suitcase, all right, but it's only got one destination on it —London. If she'd been touring all over the country, this would be full of the names of the cities she's visited."

Patch and Rolly dashed over to the bag. But in his excitement Rolly stumbled headlong into the suitcase, and it clattered loudly as it rocked back and forth. Aunt Ida came running. Quickly she opened the bag, looked inside, and closed it again before Nanny reached the room.

"No harm done, Nanny," she smiled. "One of your puppies must have knocked it over." They went back to the kitchen.

"Did you see that?" yelped Lucky excitedly. "That bag was loaded with valuable china. I bet Aunt Ida is a cat burglar. She gets into people's homes with a made-up story about being someone's aunt and robs them at night when they're asleep."

"Oh, no!" cried Patch. "What should we do now?"

"You know, Lucky," said Pongo gently, "it's okay to be suspicious of strangers, but it's really not a very good idea to jump to conclusions."

"I guess you're right," said Lucky. "But there's still one mystery we haven't solved."

"What's that?" asked his father.

"Why didn't Anita ever get the card telling her Aunt Ida was coming?"

"Someone—a puppy perhaps—may have intercepted the mail," said his mother.

"You mean one of us chewed up the postcard?" asked Lucky.

"Precisely," she said.

Rolly interrupted. "Was it a pretty picture card that smelled like flowers?" he asked, looking guilty.

"Oh, Rolly!" sighed Lucky.

"I was hungry!" Rolly said.

"Well," said Lucky, "it was fun being a detective for one night."

His father grinned. "And on a dark and stormy night, at that!"

"We'll take turns standing guard outside her door. If she gets up during the night, we'll bark." The other two puppies agreed.

When Roger and Anita returned in the morning with Pongo and Perdita, they found twelve of their puppies asleep in a warm basket by the stove. And they found Lucky, Patch, and Rolly sound asleep in front of the door to Aunt Ida's room.

Later, Lucky told his mother and father all about the strange Aunt Ida and why they had decided to sleep by her door.

"There's a simple explanation for everything," said Perdita. "Aunt Ida told Anita she bought the dishes just before she arrived. She had to buy a new suitcase to carry them, so the tag only said 'London.'"

"Well, what about the English clothes?" asked Lucky.

"She bought the coat and boots here," said his mother.

COMPUTERS
OF THE FUTURE

It's a Wednesday night in the year 2001, and you sit down at your computer to do your homework. "How may I help you?" the machine drawls in a soft Southern accent.

"I have to do a report on the Boston Tea Party," you say. "But I'd rather play a video game."

"I'm sorry, but games cannot be accessed until 8 p.m.," the computer replies. "I can provide the following material on the Boston Tea Party." The computer screen then flashes a list that includes four encyclopedia articles, a recent magazine piece, and a tele-

vision documentary. You lightly touch the screen and choose the documentary.

As the TV show plays on the computer screen, you stop it from time to time to dictate notes to the computer. When the documentary ends, the computer speaks again.

"I have the information on baseball tickets that you requested this morning. Would you like to review it now?"

This scene isn't as far-fetched as it may seem. Today's computers are more powerful than ever—some can already speak and present recorded video material. The reason is that designers have vastly increased the memory of computers—and with it, their ability to store and process information.

One result is that the personal computer, or PC, has become the workhorse of the computer world. In recent years it has taken over jobs that only huge computers could do in the past. PC's range from desktop models to portables, some of which weigh as little as a pound. All are vastly smaller, less expensive, and faster than earlier computers.

At the same time, large computers have also increased their capabilities. Today's large computers are supercomputers, able to handle vast amounts of information and perform calculations with blazing speed.

Large and small, computers are being used in more ways than ever before. And the computers of tomorrow promise to have even more capabilities.

NEW IMAGES

Traditionally, computers have excelled in performing complicated mathematical calculations, keeping records, and handling written information. Now they are beginning to handle images in much the same way.

Improvements in computer graphics techniques allow the machines to create full-color pictures that are as realistic as photographs. Some systems can produce motion and the appearance of depth on the screen. And a technique called document imaging allows actual documents and photographs to be entered directly into a computer.

Most of these image-processing techniques aren't new, but in the past they required high-powered and expensive computer systems. Now, more and more of them can be performed by smaller and more affordable computers. At the same time, the quality of computer images has improved vastly. This has made them useful in many different fields.

Publishers can combine words with pictures and produce material entirely by computer. Manufacturers can use computer graphics to design new products and even new factories. And instead of being buried by mounds of paper, offices can set up "electronic filing cabinets" by scanning documents and storing them in computers.

Mapmakers are also turning to computers. Computerized mapmaking systems can combine images with a wealth of information from census reports and other sources—everything from the location of power lines to the number of houses on a street. The most complex mapmaking systems are being developed by governments. But businesses are using these methods to produce customized maps that help them calculate the best shipping routes and pinpoint the best locations for new facilities.

Computer graphics are especially helpful in scientific and technical fields because complex subjects can be quickly understood through pictures. And computers can produce pictures of things that would otherwise be difficult or impossible to see.

In hospitals, for example, surgeons can plan their operations by examining three-dimensional images of structures inside the human body. In research laboratories, chemists can use computer graphics to produce pictures of molecules that are far too small to be seen. And geologists can create three-dimensional models of rock formations hidden deep in the earth—to find, for example, a likely spot to drill for oil.

Sports scientists can use computer imaging to analyze an athlete's performance. First the performance is videotaped. A series of images showing the athlete at different points in the performance is transferred from the tape to the computer. On the computer, the scientist "marks" key spots on the athlete's body. And the computer uses these points to produce a stick figure that can be studied at every stage of movement.

By combining graphics with the power of a supercomputer, astronomers can produce pictures of events that otherwise could only be imagined, such as the birth of a galaxy or the death of a star. Many such events can't be observed—galaxies formed billions of years ago, and a star's life span is measured in millions of years. But a supercomputer can analyze these enormously complicated processes, compress the time scale, and produce full-color simulations of the events.

High-powered imaging and mapmaking systems are still very expensive. But some PC's already have many computer imaging capabilities. Computer designers say that in the near future, image processing will be a standard feature, even on home computers.

TALK TO ME

How about a computer that can carry on a conversation—talk to you, and understand what you say? Such machines may be commonplace in the not-too-distant future.

Computer designers have already made great strides in voice simulation, the ability of computers to reproduce the human voice. Early systems produced sounds that were more like electronic squawks than human speech. Now computers can produce pleasant voices and even duplicate regional accents and the speech of famous people.

Using sophisticated computer graphics, sports scientists can analyze an athlete's every leap, step, and vault.

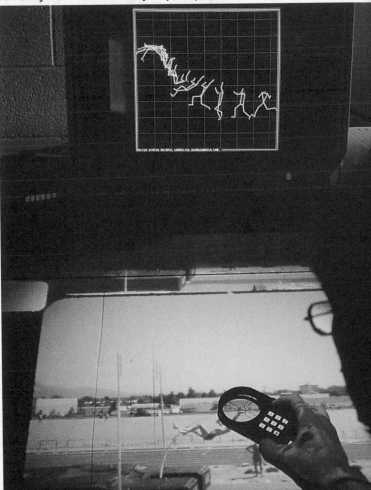

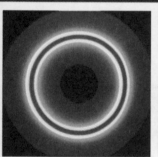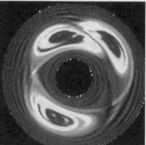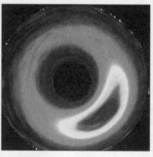

Astronomers can combine graphics with the power of a supercomputer and produce pictures of events that otherwise could only be imagined. Shown at the left is a simulation of the formation of Jupiter's Great Red Spot, an atmospheric storm.

Talking computers are expected to become important tools in teaching—especially in teaching foreign languages. Students will be able to type words on their computers and hear the computer "read" them with the correct pronunciation.

The ability of computers to reproduce sound will affect other areas. People will play, study, and compose music on computers. And when sound reproduction is combined with the latest computer graphics techniques, video games will rival feature films—with stereo sound tracks and realistic special effects.

Getting a computer to *understand* speech has proved more difficult than reproducing sound. The best speech-recognition systems can understand only about a thousand words. Partly, this is because the pronunciation of words varies depending on who is speaking. The computer may not recognize a word if there is even a slight variation in the way it is pronounced. But when a computer is "trained" to recognize just one person's voice, it can handle a larger vocabulary.

Computer experts expect these problems to be solved. And when they are, computers may be controlled entirely by voice commands. They will even take dictation.

COMPUTERS AND VIDEO

With their improved graphics and sound, computers are being linked with another new technology: the videodisc. And the combination has exciting possibilities.

Compact discs that hold written information have been used with computers for several years. With a special attachment, the computer can read the information on the disc and display it on the screen. An entire encyclopedia can fit on a single disc.

With videodiscs, however, the computer can display still pictures and full-motion video as well as words. A 12-inch disc holds tens of thousands of still pictures or well over an hour of full-motion video. You can tell the computer to call up any photo or any segment of the video. The screens in computer-videodisc systems produce pictures that are even sharper than those of standard television sets.

Computer-videodisc systems are being used in some schools, and some companies are using them to train employees. Teachers say that students learn faster with the systems—because the students are in control.

Suppose, for example, that you want to learn about cell division. A textbook can explain the process and show diagrams and photographs. A filmstrip or videotape can show actual cells dividing. A computer-videodisc system can do all that, too. And if you have a question or are confused at any point, you can stop the presentation to call up more information or to review what you've seen. The computer can also ask questions, to see if you've understood the material. If you give a wrong answer, it will give you more information in that area.

Someday the contents of entire libraries—not just books but pictures, recordings, and filmstrips—may be stored on videodiscs. People will use computers to get the information they want. To find out about a famous painting, for example, you might ask the computer to show you a high-quality reproduction of the picture, written material about it, and a video on the artist.

Computer-videodisc systems may eventually be found in homes, where they will be hooked up to television sets. At the touch of a button, people will be able to call up information to supplement what they see broadcast on television—background on a country that's featured on the evening news, or a full account of a historical event that's the subject of a miniseries.

NEW JOBS FOR COMPUTERS

As PC's become ever more powerful, they will be able to perform many jobs at once. While you are using your computer to type a letter or research a report, for example, the machine may also be tapping into a ticket reservation system to book seats for you and your friends at an upcoming rock concert.

Computers will take on new roles, too. The house of the future may be run by a computer that can do everything from turn on the lights to water the lawn.

An experimental home system like this has already been built. In it, a computer operates the home's electric, heating, and other

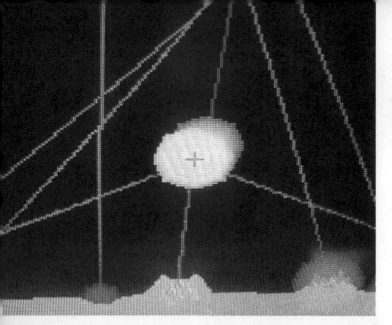

systems. All the lights and other equipment can be turned on and off from a central control panel, which features a touch-sensitive video screen. If you want to turn on the stereo, you just put your finger on the right spot on the screen.

Sensors keep track of temperature and automatically adjust the heat, report if someone is moving through a room, and indicate if the oven was left on. If an appliance breaks, the computer can even tell what went wrong. A voice-recognition system locks and unlocks doors at a spoken command. And moisture detectors buried in the ground outside turn on the sprinklers when the lawn is dry.

COMPUTING WITH LIGHT

The reason that computers have become more powerful even as they have grown smaller is that more and more of their electronic circuitry has been squeezed onto tiny silicon chips. Computer designers are working on even better chips. But sometime in the next century, the most powerful computers of all may have no electronic circuits and no silicon chips. Instead of electrical current, they will use pulses of light to do their work.

Experimental optical computers, as such devices are called, have already been built. They contain networks of lasers, mirrors, and lenses. As the machine makes its calculations, beams of laser light are focused and directed through the network by the lenses and mirrors. (Ordinary light contains light waves of many different lengths, which scatter in all directions. In laser light, the light waves are all the same length, and they travel together in a narrow beam.) The beams can be switched on and off as many as a billion times a second, which will give optical computers enormous speed.

Researchers say that when optical computers are perfected—perhaps sometime early in the 21st century—they will be a thousand times faster than the most powerful machines of today. They will be able to store vast amounts of information, and they may be able to perform millions of tasks at once. When that happens, you'll be able to finish your homework with the speed of light!

As computers have become more powerful, computer games have advanced. Early games (*top*) showed pictures that were simple and boxy-looking; more recent games (*center*) show more detailed pictures; some of today's games show images that have almost an artistic quality (*bottom*).

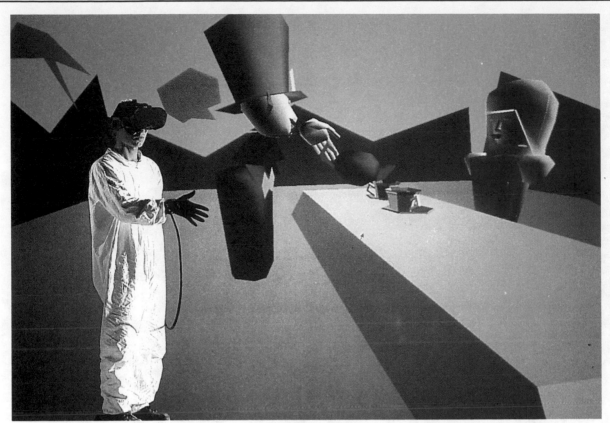

A computerized mask and glove allow you to enter the three-dimensional world of "virtual reality."

SUPER SIMULATIONS

Imagine playing a game of tennis right in your living room—or exploring Mars without leaving Earth. Both may be possible one day, through advanced computer simulations.

Computer simulations are already being used as training tools, mainly for airplane pilots. A flight simulator can mimic the sights, sounds, and sensations of flying a plane so realistically that it's hard to believe you're still on the ground.

From outside, the simulator is a big box on legs. Inside is a cockpit that is accurate down to the last gauge and switch. The windscreen shows a realistic view of ground and sky. And the whole box tilts and shifts as the simulator "flies." All the action is controlled by a computer. It responds to the pilot's actions. And it sets up emergency situations—a failed engine, for example—in order to test the pilot's reactions.

Another computer simulation puts medical students in the middle of a hectic emergency room. The student watches a computer-controlled video screen and has to make decisions on how to treat a patient with a gunshot wound. If the student makes the wrong decision, the patient "dies"— but fortunately, the patient is just an actor.

As realistic as these simulations are, they are crude compared to the systems that computer experts are now developing. New technology is able to create an environment called artificial or "virtual" reality. In one system, you need a computerized mask and glove. The mask has two tiny video screens, one in front of each eye. It is connected to a computer, which contains a special program. When you put the mask on, you're transported into a three-dimensional simulated world. And when you move your head up or down or sideways, the view changes.

The computerized glove allows you to interact with this artificial world. It contains sensors that report the position and movements of your hand. If you reach out to touch something in your artificial world, an image of a hand appears in front of your eyes and actually performs the action.

Researchers expect to develop ever more realistic video displays for these advanced simulations. Some are developing full body suits filled with sensors like those in the gloves. And virtual environments may one day be widely used, for recreation as well as training. People could explore exotic places and even distant planets, or even play a simulated game of tennis, right in their living rooms.

SCULPTURES IN THE SAND

If you've ever been to the beach, you've probably tried your hand at building a simple fort or a castle in the sand. You may even have discovered that with a little water and a few simple tools, sand can be used to create all sorts of fanciful sculptures. Sculpting in sand is challenging and fun—so much so that sand sculpture contests have become popular events in many seaside areas. In fact, sand sculpture has become "big"—in more ways than one.

Imagine, for example, a sand castle nearly the height of a four-story building, stretching 198 feet (60 meters) along the beach. Such a castle was built at Treasure Island, Florida, a few years ago. About 1,400 volunteers worked for almost two weeks to pile and carve the 20,000 tons of wet sand that formed the castle. They worked under the direction of—believe it or not—professional sand-castle builders. The finished work, called Bluebeard's Castle, was one of the largest sand castles ever built, and it drew some 400,000 spectators.

Although the evidence has long since washed away, people have probably been modeling sand since ancient times. But as far as anyone knows, enormous and elaborate creations like Bluebeard's Castle are something new. Some are designed and built by professionals for films and promotional events. Others are built for the sand sculpture contests that are held in beachfront resorts everywhere—from Virginia Beach, Virginia, to Imperial Beach, California, to White Rock, British Columbia.

The contests are a way of drawing crowds to the resorts, and they often offer prize money to the best entries. Both amateurs and professionals compete in various categories, often working in teams. What do the sculptors build? Besides castles, nautical subjects—from sea serpents to sunken ships—are the most popular. But just about any subject might appear in the sand: telephones, televisions, and cars alongside pigs, dogs, dragons, and other real and fanciful animals. At one contest, a team led by a dentist

Sand sculpture contests are very popular today. Many of the creations are quite elaborate and detailed, and they involve careful planning. The towering castle, whimsical pig, and fanciful automobile shown on these pages drew thousands of spectators—before the sculptures were washed away by the tides.

carved a set of teeth accompanied by a toothbrush and a tube of toothpaste.

Sand is easy to shape and carve, but creating a large or elaborate sand structure can be tricky. First comes careful planning and design work—most sand sculptures are wider than they are tall, so that they won't tumble down too easily. Then wet sand must be piled in the rough shape of the sculpture, which is hard work if the sculpture is very large. Sometimes the sand is piled and compacted into wooden forms, which are later removed.

Finally, the sand artists carefully carve the final shape, using tools that range from putty knives to melon-ball scoops. Meanwhile, to keep the sand from drying out and crumbling away, the sculpture is dampened with a spray of water from time to time.

All this must be done quickly—because all sand sculptures have short lives. Sooner or later, the tide will come in and wash the creation away.

SAVE THE ELEPHANTS

A huge form takes shape in the dim light of an African dawn: an elephant, slowly moving toward the bank of a river. Cautiously, the great beast lifts its trunk and sniffs the air for danger. Then it rumbles a signal, and other elephants appear on the riverbank. Soon all are drinking and bathing contentedly—snorting, rolling in the mud, and playfully squirting water over themselves.

Standing about 10 feet (3 meters) tall and weighing as much as 6 tons, elephants are the largest land animals. They are famous for their intelligence as well as for their size and strength. People have long admired them—in the 1600's, the English poet John Donne called the elephant "Nature's great masterpiece" and "the only harmless great thing." Yet today these magnificent animals are in danger of disappearing forever.

Part of the threat comes from the growth of civilization: Much of the elephants' natural habitat has been taken over by people for use as farm and grazing land. Even more serious, however, is the widespread slaughter of elephants by hunters. Most of the animals are killed for one reason—their ivory tusks, which are valued for making jewelry and other items.

Now, however, people are taking action to save the elephants. The steps include new efforts to protect the animals from poachers and an international ban on ivory trade, which was adopted by many countries late in 1989.

A MAJESTIC ANIMAL

There are two kinds of elephants: African elephants, which live in parts of Africa south of the Sahara, and Asian elephants, which live in India, Sri Lanka, and Southeast Asia. And there are a number of differences between them.

African elephants are larger and have bigger ears and flatter heads than their Asian cousins, for example. The back of the Asian elephant is convex, or arched, while the African elephant has a dip behind the shoulders. And African bulls (males) and cows (females) both have well-developed tusks, which are actually enormous curving teeth. Asian bulls and cows have only short tusks, and many cows have none at all.

There are differences in temperament, too. Asian elephants have long been tamed by people and used as riding and work animals. In the past, they were used in battle. Today they are still used as work animals, mainly in logging—an elephant can drag two tons and lift 600 pounds (270 kilograms) with its trunk and tusks. And Asian elephants are the elephants you see in the circus. African elephants, on the other hand, are wilder and are rarely tamed.

Despite these differences, wild Asian and African elephants live in much the same way. Most elephants travel in herds of ten to fifty individuals, roaming over a wide area in search of plants to eat and water for drinking and bathing. The herd is made up mostly of cows and young elephants, or calves. Adult males generally travel alone, and when two meet, they may fight.

An elephant eats constantly, consuming as much as 500 pounds (225 kilograms) of food a day. The animals can strip bark from trees with their tusks and even uproot trees to get at the tasty green leaves. In this way, herds of elephants help keep the African plains open and free of brush. They also use their great tusks to dig open water holes. This is helpful to the other grasslands animals.

An elephant herd is led by an experienced cow. This cow and the other older females, or matriarchs, teach the younger ones how to find food and water, what migration routes to take, and other important elephant knowledge. Calves live with the group as long as fourteen years, learning these skills.

The members of the herd are usually related, and they form a closely knit group. Mothers make sure their babies keep up as the herd travels, using their trunks and heads to nudge the little ones along. Other cows act as elephant aunts, helping to look out for the calves. If a calf is attacked or injured, the herd will gather around to defend or help it. The concern that elephants show for others of their kind is one of the traits that has endeared them to people.

ELEPHANTS IN DANGER

While Asian elephants have been considered endangered animals since the early 1970's, concern for African elephants has grown recently. By some estimates, the number of African elephants was cut in half between 1979 and 1989, shrinking from nearly 1.3 million to about 625,000. At this rate, some people think, African elephants will be wiped out in another twenty years.

What's behind their dwindling numbers? In many areas of Africa, elephants range over land that's needed for agriculture. A herd of elephants moving through a farmer's fields can destroy crops in short order. Thus farmers see the animals as huge pests, and they shoot them or drive them away.

To protect the animals, many African countries have set aside reserves for elephants. By law, the animals may not be killed in the reserves. And the killing of animals that wander off the reserves is limited by law.

In most places, however, the elephant herds have shrunk dramatically in spite of the reserves and laws that are supposed to protect them. And the main reason is that poachers (illegal hunters) have continued to kill the animals for their ivory.

The poachers use military-style automatic weapons to kill the great beasts. They especially hunt the bulls, which have the biggest tusks. This affects the entire elephant population—as the number of bulls declines, the

Young elephants live with members of the herd for many years. They learn how to survive from the more mature females. Thus when the older elephants are slaughtered by hunters, the young elephants may never learn how to find food and water.

cows have fewer opportunities for mating, and so there are fewer calves.

When poachers can no longer find enough bulls, they turn their guns on the mature females in the herds. Often they mow down entire groups of elephants, young and old, simply to get the large tusks of the matriarchs. By some estimates, poachers kill about 200 African elephants a day.

When a herd is attacked by poachers, even the elephants that escape the bullets may not survive. When a mother elephant is killed, for example, her baby will starve or die of thirst before it will leave her side. And when the most mature and experienced matriarchs of a herd are killed, the younger elephants may never learn how to find good water holes and food sources.

The poachers have continued this slaughter because of the great demand for ivory. The tusks of a single elephant can bring more money than many Africans earn in a year. Most of the tusks are smuggled out of Africa to Hong Kong and other places in the Far East, where the demand is especially high. There the ivory is carved into all kinds of items, from sculpture and jewelry to buttons, dice, and piano keys.

Concern about the fate of the elephants caused a number of countries, including the United States, Canada, most Western European nations, and Japan, to halt imports of ivory in mid-1989. And later that year, 76 countries backed an agreement banning trade in ivory. At the same time, they named the African elephant an endangered species. The ban caused an immediate drop in the demand for ivory.

Some countries refused to go along with the ivory ban. These were mostly countries such as Zimbabwe and Botswana, where the elephants have been well protected. In fact, the animals are so well protected that the herds sometimes grow too large. Too many elephants damage the environment, stripping the land of vegetation and making food scarce for all animals. Then the government must ''cull the herds''—kill some of the elephants—to protect the environment.

These countries aren't wealthy, and they would like to sell the ivory from their *legally* hunted elephants. But many people worry

that the buyers of ivory won't bother to ask how it was obtained. Thus, they say, poaching and smuggling will continue as long as *any* trade in ivory is allowed.

The ivory ban is to last until 1992, when the countries involved will review it. Meanwhile, African countries are taking other steps to protect the elephants. They are stepping up patrols against poachers and cracking down on corrupt officials who have closed their eyes to ivory smuggling. Some are fencing off reserves in areas where elephants come in conflict with farmers. And wildlife groups are spreading the word about the dangers the animals face, urging people not to buy ivory items. Their hope is that the magnificent elephant can be saved.

THE CIVIL WAR
An Anniversary Album

In all of American history, perhaps no chapter is darker than that of the Civil War, the bitter conflict between the North and the South. The war broke out in 1861, after a number of Southern states seceded, or withdrew, from the Union. It ended four years later, in April, 1865, when Southern forces surrendered to the North. The year 1990 marked the 125th anniversary of the end of the war, which had caused enormous pain on both sides. (Above: Large areas of Georgia were left devastated by a Northern army under General William Tecumseh Sherman, which cut a swath of destruction from Atlanta to the sea in 1864.)

The issues that tore the country in two in 1861 were slavery and states' rights. These issues had been simmering for a long time. Since Colonial times, the Southern economy had been based on large plantations that were worked by slaves. In the North, farms were smaller, so there was little need for slave labor. The North also developed manufacturing and other industries earlier than the South. By the early 1800's, slavery had been outlawed in most of the North.

Many Northerners believed that slavery was immoral and shouldn't be allowed in the western territories that were then seeking statehood. Some thought that it should be abolished completely. But in the South, most people felt that each state should decide the question of slavery for itself. And they believed that slavery was essential to their way of life. Southerners disagreed with Northerners on other issues, too. But slavery was the issue that provoked the most passionate disagreement.

In the mid-1850's, the divisions between the North and the South grew deeper. The question of whether the territory of Kansas should enter the Union as a slave or free state led to bitter debates in Congress—and bloodshed between pro- and anti-slavery groups in the territory. Meanwhile, abolitionists—people who wanted to abolish, or end, slavery—were gaining support in the North. Harriet Beecher Stowe's novel *Uncle Tom's Cabin* (advertised in the poster at right), published in 1852, presented a picture of suffering slaves that won many people to the abolitionist cause. In 1859, the abolitionist John Brown tried to start a slave rebellion. The attempt failed and Brown was hanged. But the incident increased the split between Northerners, who saw Brown as a hero, and Southerners, who saw him as a dangerous criminal.

135,000 SETS, 270,000 VOLUMES SOLD.

UNCLE TOM'S CABIN

FOR SALE HERE.

AN EDITION FOR THE MILLION, COMPLETE IN 1 Vol., PRICE 37 1-2 CENTS.
" " IN GERMAN, IN 1 Vol., PRICE 50 CENTS.
" " IN 2 Vols,. CLOTH, 6 PLATES, PRICE $1.50.
SUPERB ILLUSTRATED EDITION, IN 1 Vol., WITH 153 ENGRAVINGS,
PRICES FROM $2.50 TO $5.00.

The Greatest Book of the Age.

By 1860 there were about 4 million slaves, making up nearly a third of the South's population. Originally, slaves that worked the Southern plantations were imported from Africa. As public feeling against slavery grew, the United States banned the importation of slaves in 1808. However, slaves were still bought and sold within the country, often at slave auctions such as the one shown below.

In 1858, the issue of slavery was taken up by two candidates in a race for a U.S. Senate seat in Illinois. They were Senator Stephen Douglas and Abraham Lincoln, a lawyer and former congressman. In seven debates around the state, Douglas presented the case for each state's right to decide the issue. Lincoln called slavery an evil that was harming blacks, whites, and the entire country.

The Lincoln-Douglas debates drew national attention. Lincoln lost the senatorial election, but his name became well known all over the country. In 1860, the Republican Party, which opposed slavery, chose him as its presidential candidate. The Democratic Party split, with Northern Democrats choosing Stephen Douglas as their candidate and Southern Democrats supporting John C. Breckinridge. Lincoln, who had been born in a log cabin in Kentucky, had wide appeal in the North. The Republicans presented him as Honest Abe, a homespun man of the people. On November 6, Lincoln won the election, sweeping the Northern states.

Many Southerners were outraged by Lincoln's election. Although he hadn't proposed banning slavery, they believed he would do so. In December, 1860, South Carolina became the first state to secede from the Union. It was quickly followed by Alabama, Mississippi, Florida, Georgia, and Louisiana. These states formed a separate nation: the Confederate States of America. Jefferson Davis (*right*) was named president. (Five more states—Texas, Virginia, North Carolina, Tennessee, and Arkansas—later joined the Confederacy.) Feelings were so strong that Lincoln received death threats and had to travel in secrecy to Washington, D.C., for his inauguration on March 4, 1861.

Lincoln hoped that war could be avoided. But matters came to a crisis within two weeks of his inauguration. Fort Sumter, at the entrance to Charleston harbor in South Carolina, was still under Union control but was running out of supplies. When a supply fleet sent by Lincoln approached the fort on April 12, 1861, Confederate forces opened fire. Fort Sumter fell to the South within two days, and the Civil War was under way. (Below: The Confederate flag flies over Fort Sumter.)

Recruits, like the young Georgia soldier at left, flocked to the banners of both sides. At first, the South had several victories. One of the most important was the first Battle of Bull Run (or Manassas), in which Confederate forces routed Northern soldiers just a few miles from Washington, D.C., in July, 1861. Defeats such as this made people in the North realize that the war would be long and hard. President Lincoln began to assemble the largest fighting force that the country had ever seen. In all, throughout the four years of the war, more than 2 million men took up arms—more than 1.5 million for the North and 900,000 for the South.

Among the soldiers who fought for the North were nearly 200,000 blacks. Many were former slaves who had escaped through a system of hiding places called the Underground Railroad. Although they were often discriminated against, in pay and other ways, they fought courageously. (Below: Black and white soldiers on the field at the Battle of Olustee, Florida, 1864.)

There was fighting at sea, too. Northern ships blockaded Southern ports, disrupting shipping and weakening the South economically. One of the most famous naval battles of the Civil War took place on March 9, 1862, between the USS *Monitor* and the CSS *Virginia* (formerly the *Merrimack*). Neither was a clear winner, but the battle was the first between ironclads—ships with metal-covered hulls.

Between battles, soldiers like those shown below relaxed in camp. Army life involved many hardships, including pests such as lice and fleas and, above all, disease. In the Union armies, disease accounted for seven of every ten deaths; the number was even higher in the South. As the war continued, Confederate soldiers also had more and more difficulty obtaining supplies.

By the President of the United States of America

A Proclamation

I, Abraham Lincoln, President of the United States of America, and Commander-in-Chief of the Army and Navy thereof, do hereby proclaim and declare that hereafter, as heretofore, the war will be prosecuted for the object of practically restoring the constitutional relation between the United States, and each of the states, and the people thereof, in which states that relation is, or may be suspended, or disturbed.

That it is my purpose, upon the next meeting of Congress to again recommend the adoption of a practical measure tendering pecuniary aid to

In the fall of 1862, Lincoln took an important step: He issued the Emancipation Proclamation, which freed slaves in the Confederate states and took effect in January, 1863. Because the North didn't control the South, not many slaves were freed immediately. But the proclamation strengthened the Northern cause, and it established an important principle. The Thirteenth Amendment to the Constitution, which became law just after the war, outlawed slavery forever throughout the United States. (Left: A draft of the Emancipation Proclamation in Lincoln's handwriting.)

The long, bitter war came to an end in 1865. Union armies had driven deep into the South. In early April, they captured Richmond, Virginia, the Confederate capital. Southern forces tried to retreat but were surrounded by Union troops. On April 9, the Confederate forces surrendered to the North at Appomattox Court House, Virginia. (Right: The surrender was made by one of the South's greatest military leaders, General Robert E. Lee, shown standing on the left in this picture. It was accepted by the famous Northern General Ulysses S. Grant, shown on the right.)

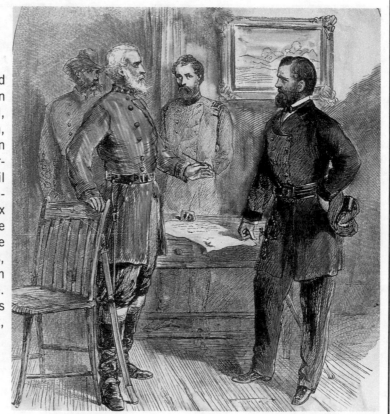

Just five days after the surrender at Appomattox, tragedy struck the nation. On the evening of April 14, President Lincoln went to Ford's Theatre in Washington to see a play. Suddenly a shadowy figure entered the president's booth, pulled a gun, and shot Lincoln in the head. The president died just after dawn the next morning. His assassin was John Wilkes Booth, an actor who had been a strong supporter of the South.

The president's death caused an outpouring of grief. Lincoln had just been elected to a second term, and many people had counted on his leadership in healing the deep national wounds caused by the war. The Civil War had established the supremacy of the federal government over the states, and it had freed the slaves. But the cost had been enormous—by some estimates, 620,000 Americans died in the war, more than in World War I and World War II and Vietnam combined. Even when the fighting stopped, much remained to be done. The economy of the South had been shattered by the war, and the old Southern way of life was gone. And while blacks were freed from slavery, they were only beginning what would prove to be a long, difficult struggle for civil rights and equality.

Still, the Union had been preserved. And in the years that followed, the country was able to put the bitterness of the Civil War behind it and begin one of its greatest periods of growth and expansion.

THE WATER WITCH

Once there was a place called Green Valley. It was the greenest, richest valley in all the kingdom. Green Valley was blessed with fair weather and the perfect mixture of sunny skies and gentle rain all year long. The people who lived in Green Valley were happy to live in such a wonderful place.

The children of Green Valley were happy, too, especially Calvin, Marvin, Melvin, and their little sister, Bitsy. They called themselves the Junior Knights, and they played all day at Great Adventures.

King Leo the Lazy lived in the big castle on the hill. Every day his generous subjects brought baskets, barrels, boxes, and bushels of delicious food as gifts to the king. King Leo grew fat, happy, and even lazier.

Then, one season, the rain was late. The farmers in Green Valley waited for the rain to water the seeds they had planted. They waited, and waited, and waited some more. Still no rain came.

King Leo the Lazy waited, too, but the baskets and barrels and boxes and bushels of food didn't arrive. King Leo grew thin and mean—although he was still very lazy.

The weeks without rain turned into months without rain, and then into an entire season without rain. The town well dried up, and so did the lake. Things got so bad that King Leo the Lazy and his court packed up their belongings and moved away, searching for a more prosperous kingdom over which to rule.

Calvin, Marvin, Melvin, and Bitsy, the Junior Knights, were sad to see King Leo and his knights leave. They feared there would be no more Great Adventures.

One day an old man came to Green Valley. "I can find water," he told the amazed townspeople.

The Junior Knights listened as the old man showed the townspeople a strange forked stick. He said that the stick would point to water that was under the ground.

There was hope in Green Valley as the old

man walked over town and farm, field and forest, waiting for his stick to twitch and tell him there was water under the ground.

But day after day, nothing happened. The townspeople were about to give up hope, when suddenly the stick began to twitch and jump and wiggle. "Water!" shouted the old man.

The stick vibrated and hummed as it pointed to a purple hill overlooking Green Valley. Then, all at once, the stick crumbled to pieces. The pieces dropped to the dust.

"It's the sign of the Water Witch. She must live in that hill up there," said the old man. "She's the one who has stolen the water of Green Valley. If you want the water back, you must offer her a gift."

"What kind of gift?" asked Bitsy.

"No one knows," the old man answered, shaking his head sadly.

That afternoon the people of Green Valley

held a meeting to decide what to offer the Water Witch. The meeting went on far into the night, but they couldn't reach any decision. The next morning, the grown-ups were still arguing.

"They'll be arguing forever," said Calvin, "and there's no time to waste."

So the Junior Knights slipped away and began hiking to the Water Witch's mountain. At the top of the mountain they found the entrance to what looked like a small cave. "This must be it," said Melvin. "Are you scared?"

"Yes," said Calvin.

"Yes," said Marvin.

"Yes," said Bitsy. "But not too scared to try to save Green Valley."

"Remember—this is a Great Adventure," Calvin said bravely.

They walked into the cave and found themselves standing on a narrow ledge. To their amazement, they saw that they were in a huge cavern, which was dripping with water.

"I haven't seen so much water in a year!" exclaimed Calvin.

The floor of the cavern was a lake, with huge waves crashing against the sides. In the middle of the lake was an island.

In the middle of the island stood the Water Witch. She was blue from head to toe, but unlike the beautiful blue of the water, hers was an ugly, mean-looking blue. And the Water Witch was an ugly, mean-looking witch.

"Visitors! How nice!" said the Water Witch, gazing up at the children. Then she waved her hand and the Junior Knights were whisked in a flash onto her island.

"Have a drink of water," offered the Water Witch. "It will probably be your last!"

The Junior Knights gulped hard. Then Calvin stepped forward. "Water Witch, we'd like our water back," he said politely.

"I'll bet you would," answered the Water Witch. "What will you offer me?"

"My father's sword," said Calvin. He held out the shiny sword.

"What use have I for a sword?" asked the Water Witch. She pointed her finger and the sword turned to rust and crumbled in Calvin's hand.

The Water Witch laughed nastily. Then she turned to Marvin. "What will *you* offer me?" she asked.

Marvin rolled his eyes and swallowed hard. "Well, the girls in Green Valley say that I am very handsome," said Marvin. "So I will offer you a kiss." He closed both eyes and puckered up. But instead of kissing him, the Water Witch threw a bucket of cold water in his face. "I wouldn't kiss the likes of you!" she shrieked.

Then she turned to Melvin. "What will *you* offer me?" Melvin reached in his backpack and pulled out a piggy bank. "All my money—every last cent," said Melvin. He shook the bank so the Water Witch could hear the coins inside.

The Water Witch shook with laughter, splashing water on Melvin. "Money means nothing to me! I have more money than you could ever dream of!" Now she turned to Bitsy. "And what about *you*, little girl?" she asked.

Slowly, Bitsy reached in her purse and pulled out a tattered old rag doll with one eye missing. "This is Esmerelda. She's my favorite thing in the whole world," said Bitsy.

The Water Witch howled with laughter. "A doll! I wouldn't give up my water for a doll! Now be off with you, all of you!"

The Junior Knights sadly turned to leave the cave.

Suddenly, Bitsy turned back to the Water Witch. "Here. You can keep Esmerelda, even if you didn't give us the water."

The Water Witch was shocked. "Why?" she asked.

A tear rolled down Bitsy's cheek. "Because I feel sorry for you, living all alone in this cave without any friends. Esmerelda can be your friend," she explained.

The Water Witch said nothing as she reached out to take the doll. The moment she touched Esmerelda, she changed from an ugly blue hag to a beautiful blue princess.

"Oh, thank you!" the princess exclaimed. "Years ago, an evil wizard put the Curse of the Water Witch on me. The only thing that could break the curse was an act of true caring. But few people care for a Water Witch. How can I ever thank you?"

The Junior Knights looked at one another. Then all together they shouted, "You can give us the water!"

"Gladly," the princess laughed.

It only took a day for the people of Green Valley to dig a hole through the mountain. Soon a waterfall streamed down the side of the mountain into a huge lake. The water quenched their thirst, watered their crops, floated their boats, and provided beauty for the whole land.

The princess moved into the castle abandoned by King Leo the Lazy and was loved by everyone in Green Valley.

The townspeople built a statue of Bitsy and her doll, to honor the little girl who had saved the town. It's all still there: Green Valley, the castle, the waterfall, the lakes, the houses, and the statue. It's all still there—if you can find it.

THE COUNTING OF AMERICA

On April 1, 1990, the United States sat for a national family portrait. It was census day —the day on which the U.S. government attempts to count every man, woman, and child in the country.

The 1990 census was the twenty-first such head count undertaken in the United States. It was also the largest ever—the government tried to reach some 250 million people. What did the government want to know? Beyond mere numbers, the 1990 census was designed to provide a detailed picture of the United States—who its people are, where they're from, and where and how they live.

THE REASONS FOR THE COUNT

The original purpose of the U.S. census was to ensure that everyone is properly represented in the House of Representatives, and this is still a main goal. Every state is guaranteed at least one seat in the House. The rest of the 435 seats are divided up among the states on the basis of their populations, using census figures that are taken decennially (every ten years). After each census, the seats are re-apportioned, or divided up again, to reflect changes in population.

Census figures are also used to draw the boundaries of Congressional voting districts, so that each district will have roughly the same number of people. This helps ensure that everyone is represented equally in Congress. And state and local governments use the census figures to redraw the boundaries of their own legislative districts.

Census information also helps determine how billions of dollars in federal funds will be used each year. Federal programs that provide aid for everything from highway construction to school lunches use census figures to find out which areas are most in need of funds.

Towns, civic groups, businesses, and individuals use the figures, too. For example, census figures showing the number of preschool children in your town could help the town decide if a new school will be needed. And census figures help businesses know where to build new stores for potential shoppers and which locations will be able to provide workers for new manufacturing plants.

HOW THE CENSUS WAS TAKEN

Although April 1 was the official census day, the actual count began earlier in the year and went on for many months after that date. In late March, the Census Bureau (the government agency in charge of the census) mailed questionnaires to 88 million homes. Census workers delivered the forms in person to another 18 million households in remote areas, such as parts of the Deep South and the western mountains. To locate all the households and keep track of the millions of addresses, the bureau used some 500 powerful minicomputers. For the first time, computers also generated about 7 million maps for use in taking the census.

Most households received a short questionnaire that took about fifteen minutes to fill out. But about one of every six households received a longer form that asked detailed questions about housing, income, education, disabilities, and so on. Most people were instructed to mail the forms back to the Census Bureau by June 1, the official deadline. In some cases, census workers went to homes and retrieved the forms.

The bureau also made special efforts to count groups of people who had often been overlooked in past censuses. On the night of March 20–21, for example, 15,000 census workers fanned out across the country to find homeless people. They called at shelters for the homeless and also checked parks, subway stations, all-night movie theaters, and other places where homeless people often camp.

Almost immediately, however, it was clear that the 1990 census was running into problems. Some 4.8 million forms were returned by the Postal Service, marked "undeliverable." The bureau's mailing list also left out entire city blocks, several zip-code areas, and even two whole towns (Ross, California, and Raymond, Mississippi). By many estimates, only a fraction of the homeless were reached. And by late April, the bureau had received only 63 percent of the forms back, far fewer than it expected. It appeared that many people weren't responding to the count.

Even though people were required by law to complete and return the forms, they had many reasons for not doing so. Many tossed out the form by mistake, thinking it was a piece of junk mail. Others couldn't read the form because they couldn't speak English. Some people found the form, especially the long form, too confusing or too time-consuming to fill out. Still others felt that the questions on the form invaded their privacy.

The Census Bureau tried especially hard to find and count groups of people who had been overlooked in past censuses, such as the homeless.

They worried that the information they gave might be used against them in some way, even though census information is supposed to be kept confidential.

Because the census count is supposed to be as complete as possible, the Census Bureau tried to track down people who didn't return forms. It hired thousands of extra workers who combed city streets to find missed households and knocked on doors, hoping to get people to answer in person the questions they had failed to answer by mail. Even so, it was clear that the count couldn't be really complete.

The response was especially low among minority groups, poor people living in cities, and illegal aliens (foreign citizens living in the United States without official permission). This raised concern that the final results wouldn't reflect the U.S. population accurately. Similar concerns had been raised by the 1980 census—by some estimates, that count had reached more than 99 percent of whites but only about 94 percent of blacks.

Large cities claimed to have lost millions of dollars in federal aid, as well as political representation, as a result of undercounting in 1980. They expected to lose even more as a result of the problems with the 1990 census. Thus some people argued that the Census Bureau should adjust its figures, using statistical methods to estimate the number of people it had missed. But others argued that this would just lead to more errors.

In response to criticism, the Census Bureau conducted spot checks in August and October, recounting some 20 million housing units in all. The bureau also defended the accuracy of the census. While the country's fifteen largest cities claimed that their population had been undercounted by more than a million, census officials expected the spot checks to turn up no more than 200,000 missed people nationwide.

ADDING IT UP

While the debate on undercounting continued, census workers rushed to complete their work. Computers whirred around the clock to sort and add the information from the forms. By December 31, the Census Bureau was to present President George Bush with a state-by-state population report.

Long before then, however, the Census

Bureau was predicting some of the results. The predictions were based on early tabulations of census results and on surveys that the bureau takes every month. The surveys cover thousands of households, and they give the government a sort of crystal ball with which to keep abreast of changes in housing and population.

Here are some of the trends that the 1990 census was expected to show:

• Preliminary figures had put the population at about 246 million. But the final official count was 249.6 million. This was an increase of about 10 percent from 1980, the slowest rate of growth in any decade since the 1930's.

• The average size of a U.S. household would be 2.6 people, the smallest ever.

• The population of the Northeast was expected to fall behind the population of the West. States in the South and West were expected to gain seats in Congress, while those in the Northeast would lose seats.

• The early figures also showed that California would keep its place as the country's most populous state. In fact, the figures showed that California's population had grown 24 percent since 1980, accounting for nearly a quarter of the country's entire population growth.

• Much of California's growth—and much of the population growth nationally—came from immigration.

• Asian and Hispanic Americans would form two of the fastest-growing ethnic groups. The number of Asian Americans was expected to be up 70 percent, and the number of Hispanic Americans up 50 percent, from 1980.

• Rural areas were losing population faster than expected; metropolitan areas on both the East and West coasts were gaining.

• New York City would remain the largest city—a position it has held since the very first census, in 1790. But the Los Angeles region would be the fastest-growing of the country's major metropolitan areas, and Los Angeles would pass Chicago to become the second-largest city.

Would these predictions prove correct? The answer will come in 1991, as thousands of pages of detailed census reports are released. Together, the reports will provide a portrait of the United States.

WHICH STATES ARE GROWING THE FASTEST?
(Estimated percentage change in population, 1980–1990)

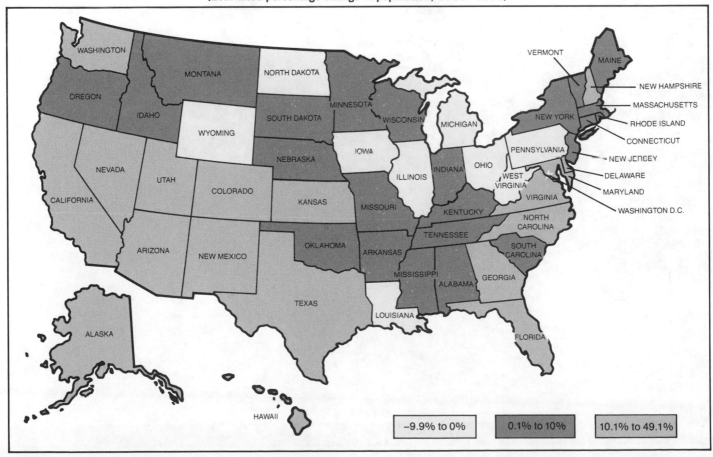

| −9.9% to 0% | 0.1% to 10% | 10.1% to 49.1% |

LEAF ART:
DON'T WASTE THEM, PASTE THEM!

Collect a variety of leaves to create insects, birds, fish, or any other type of animal—even imaginary creatures. First, dry the leaves by putting them between sheets of newspaper and placing them under a stack of heavy books for several days. Then make your design. Use glue or paste to hold each leaf in place.

ALL IN A DREAM

You're late for math class, so you rush in and quickly take a seat. The teacher gives you a cold look and hands you a paper. It's a test—and you realize with a shock that you haven't studied. What's worse, the test makes no sense—the material is so unfamiliar that you can't answer a single question. You stare at the paper, fighting a rising sense of panic. Then, suddenly, the bell rings. Class is over, and you failed the test!

But what's this? That's not the class bell. It's your alarm clock. You're not in class; you're home in bed. And you didn't fail a test—you were only dreaming.

Dreams take the real world and turn it upside down. All sorts of unpredictable and impossible things can happen: You may meet old friends who have moved far away or relatives who passed on long ago. Your pet dog may talk. You may suddenly find the solution to a problem that's been troubling you for days. Your deepest wishes may be granted—or you may be chased by a bug-eyed monster. You may even fly.

Why do we dream? Do the events in dreams have meaning? People have been fascinated by these questions since ancient times. Long ago, some people thought that dreams might be messages from the gods. Others thought that dreams were predictions of future events.

Few people hold such beliefs today. In recent times scientists have studied dreams and learned much about them. Dreams, most experts believe, are messages from our subconscious. Buried feelings and fears are called up and interwoven with events that take place during the day. But in sleep, these messages are often disguised—and that's what makes dreams so fascinating.

STUDYING DREAMS

"To sleep: perchance to dream," says the prince in Shakespeare's play *Hamlet*. Scientists say there's no chance about it: everybody dreams! Even people who say they never dream actually do—they just don't remember their dreams.

How do scientists know? They have watched people dream in sleep laboratories.

a number of sleep cycles. Each cycle lasts about 90 minutes and is made up of a period of deep sleep and a period of light sleep. Near the end of the cycle comes a period of what scientists call *r*apid *e*ye *m*ovement, or REM, sleep.

During REM sleep, a person's eyes move back and forth as if he or she were watching something. Brain waves show patterns that resemble those seen in a person who is awake. The sleeper's heart and breathing rates may increase. And by waking volunteers during REM sleep, researchers have learned that this is when most dreams occur.

Over eight hours of sleep, most people have three to five dreams, each lasting five to fifty minutes. Usually, most of the dreams are forgotten by morning. But by waking volunteers in the middle of a dream and asking them about it, researchers have learned a lot about dreams.

For example, while many people think that they dream in black and white, dreams are almost always in color. Apparently the memory of the colors in our dreams fades even more quickly than the memory of the dreams themselves.

People usually hear as well as see in their dreams. Dreams may even involve the senses of smell and touch. Blind people dream as much as sighted people, but their dreams are made up of sounds, smells, and sensations. During REM sleep, their eyes don't move.

In many dreams, the dreamer simply watches the action. In others the dreamer plays a part. While sleeping, people seldom move or act out their dreams. That's because messages from the brain to the muscles are blocked during REM sleep.

Whether we watch the action or take part in it, many of our dreams involve people and places with which we're familiar. Often, dreams seem to be related to events that took place during the day and especially the hours just before sleep. But in dreams, people may behave strangely and familiar places may be oddly changed. Events often make no sense, although during the dream they may seem logical. Other dreams, however, are so realistic that on awakening, the dreamer can't believe that the events didn't really happen.

At a sleep laboratory, volunteers are hooked up to electronic monitoring equipment. An electroencephalograph, or EEG, records brain waves—the electrical impulses that are constantly given off by the brain. Other machines monitor eye movements and heart and breathing rates.

The volunteers' job is easy—they simply go to sleep. But all night long, scientists keep watch on the monitoring equipment. Brain waves vary with the brain's activity, so watching the EEG tells scientists what's going on while the volunteer is sleeping. Heart rate and other physical signs also vary through the night.

By studying sleeping volunteers, researchers have learned that there are different kinds of sleep. Every night, you go through

Knowing these facts about dreams doesn't explain what purpose dreams serve or why people dream what they do. But researchers have plenty of theories.

THE LANGUAGE OF DREAMS

One of the best-known theories of the meaning of dreams was developed by Austrian physician Sigmund Freud, in the 1890's. Freud originated psychoanalysis, a method of helping people with emotional problems. Part of Freud's complex dream theory stated that dreams are a way in which people fulfill subconscious wishes—wishes that they don't even know they have. The wish fulfillment happens indirectly, through symbols. That is, the images in dreams stand for ideas or things that are too stressful for the dreamer to picture directly and thus must be disguised.

More recently, some researchers have proposed theories that are almost the opposite of Freud's. According to one of these theories, dreams mean nothing at all. During sleep, the cerebral cortex (the part of the brain that's involved in thought) is stimulated randomly. Thus dreams are just meaningless images, called up by chance.

Another current theory states that dreams are a sort of housecleaning mechanism—a way in which the brain gets rid of incorrect associations and patterns of thought. (If this is so, it's best to forget your dreams.) And still other researchers think that dreams serve a vital biological purpose: By activating the brain during sleep, they keep it from drifting too deeply into unconsciousness.

Most people, however, believe that dreams have at least some meaning. And while many experts disagree with parts of Freud's dream theory, it is generally agreed that the mysterious images we see in sleep are symbols. If you dream about another person, for example, he or she may represent a character trait in yourself. Animals often stand for instincts and emotions. Colors may reflect your inner feelings—bright, sharp colors may indicate intense feelings, while black may indicate sadness.

Even the dream's setting is important. A house, for example, is supposed to be a symbol of the self. The basement stands for the unconscious, while the upper floors stand for the conscious mind. If you dream about a house with a lot of empty, unused rooms, your dream may be telling you that you're not using all your talents.

Everyone's dreams are unique. But certain experiences seem to occur in almost everybody's dreams at one time or another. And these experiences, too, may have symbolic meanings.

If you dream that you are falling, for example, your dream may show that you feel insecure. If you dream that you can't find something important, such as money or a set of keys, it may show that you don't want to accept grown-up responsibility. And a dream about failing an exam may show that you feel unprepared for life's demands.

But people who interpret dreams say that a dream's true meaning depends on the dreamer. Symbols are just a starting point in decoding a dream—you have to think about the dream and decide how it relates to your situation.

Many people spend a great deal of time and effort trying to understand and interpret their dreams. Some keep dream diaries or re-create their dreams in drawings. Some visit consultants who help decode the strange language of dreams. Other people find that simply telling a dream to a friend can help. In the course of talking about it, the meaning may become clear.

Sometimes dreams can help solve problems. Supposedly, the scientist Albert Einstein found the key to his famous theory of relativity in a dream. Thus some dream experts suggest that if you are troubled by a problem that you can't solve, you should focus on it just before you go to sleep. Try to state the problem as clearly as you can. Your dreams may provide the answer.

Even if your dreams don't solve your problems or reveal deep insights about yourself, thinking about them can be fun. But what if you're one of the many people who have trouble remembering dreams?

Dream experts say to try setting your alarm clock a half hour earlier than usual, so that you can "catch" a dream. Put a pad and pencil next to your bed and jot down the dream as soon as you wake up. And before you drift off to sleep at night, repeat to yourself, "I will remember my dream!"

INDEX

ILLUSTRATION CREDITS
AND ACKNOWLEDGMENTS

14 © Dave B. Fleetham—Tom Stack & Associates

15 © Denise Tackett—Tom Stack & Associates; © Larry Lipsky—DRK Photo

17 © Stephen J. Krasemann—DRK Photo

18 © Clem Haagner—Bruce Coleman Inc.

19 © Ed Robinson—Tom Stack & Associates

20 © Fred Bavendam—Valan Photos; © Zig Leszczynski—Animals Animals

21 © Michael Fogden—DRK Photo

22– Artist, Charles Varner
25

26– Peach Reynolds
27

28 The Abby Aldrich Rockefeller Folk Art Center—Colonial Williamsburg Foundation

29 The Abby Aldrich Rockefeller Folk Art Center—Colonial Williamsburg Foundation; Collection of the Museum of American Folk Art

30– The Abby Aldrich
33 Rockefeller Folk Art Center—Colonial Williamsburg Foundation

38– © Tobey Sanford
39

40 © John P. Kelly—The Image Bank

41 © Nathan Bilow—Allsport USA

42– Jackie Geyer—Ranger
43 Rick

44 AP/Wide World

45 J. Langevin—Sygma

48 © P. Robert—Sygma

49 © Anthony Suau—Black Star

51 Artist, Michèle A. McLean

52 © Chris Luneski—Image Cascade; Theodore L. Manekin; © Chris Luneski—Image Cascade

53 Theodore L. Manekin

54 © Robert A. Tyrell

55 © Clayton A. Fogle; © Robert A. Tyrell

56 Artist, Michèle A. McLean

62 © 1989 Children's Television Workshop. Used courtesy *3–2–1 Contact* magazine

63 R. Azoury—Sipa Press; © Michael Fogden—DRK Photo

64 © M.P. Kahl—DRK Photo; © Nathan Farb

65 © W. Meltzen—Southern Stock Photos; © Stephen J. Krasemann—DRK Photo

66 © Jeffry Myers—Southern Stock Photos; © Alan Oddie—Photo Edit

67 © Thomas A. Schneider—F-Stop Pictures; © Jim Brandenburg—DRK Photos

68 © Tom Bean—DRK Photos; © Frank S. Balthis

70 Designed and created by Jenny Tesar

71 Artist, Michèle A. McLean

72– © Co Rentmeester
73

74 © Linda Hill

75– © Chad Slattery
76

77 © Paul Ruben

78 John Running—Black Star

80 © Thomas Hoepker—Magnum

82 Chesnot—SIPA Press

83 © P. Habans—Sygma

88 © Stephen Hunt—The Image Bank

89 © D. Kirkland—Sygma

90 © Philip Marcus, University of California, Berkeley, *Discover* magazine; NASA

92 © Dan McCoy—Rainbow ("Missile Command," "Super Mario Bros. II"); Courtesy Bohle Company for NEC ("Psychosis")

93 © George Steinmetz

94 © Chad Slattery

95 © Jerry Howard—Positive Images; Jerry Howard—Positive Images; © Chad Slattery

96 Stephen J. Krasemann—DRK Photo

98 Stephen J. Krasemann—DRK Photo

100 The Granger Collection

101 The Bettmann Archive; Historical Picture Service

102 Illinois State Historical Library; Culver Pictures

103 Culver Pictures; Museum of the Confederacy

104 Library of Congress; The Granger Collection

105 The Bettmann Archive; Culver Pictures

106 North Wind Picture Archive; Historical Picture Service

107 The Bettmann Archive

112 Jon A. Rembold—*Insight* magazine

114 © John Giordano—SABA

116– Designed and created
117 by Michèle A. McLean

118– John Pack
119